OTHER TITLES OF INTEREST FROM ST. LUCIE PRESS

A Roadmap for Quality Transformation in Education

New Schools for a New Century

Designing High-Performance Schools

Total Quality in Higher Education

Quality in Education: An Implementation Handbook

Creating Quality in the Classroom

Teams in Education: Creating an Integrated Approach

Continuous Improvement in Education Video Series

The Baldrige Award for Education

Mastering the Diversity Challenge: Easy On-the-Job Applications for Measurable Results

The Skills of Encouragement

Improving Service Quality: Achieving High Performance in the Public and Private Sectors

For more information about these titles call, fax or write:

St. Lucie Press
2000 Corporate Blvd., N.W.
Boca Raton, FL 33431-9868

TEL (561) 994-0555 • (800) 272-7737
FAX (800) 374-3401
E-MAIL information@slpress.com
WEB SITE http://www.slpress.com

S_{L}^{t}

Learning
by Doing

Panasonic Partnerships and

Systemic School Reform

Terry A. Clark

Richard A. Lacey

S_L^t

St. Lucie Press
Delray Beach, Florida

Contents

Acknowledgments

*T*he authors would like to thank Michael Katims and Jane Canner for preparing sections of this book. William E. Bickel, Leo Gafney, and Scott Thompson reviewed a draft manuscript and provided very valuable feedback and perspective. Much of the information in this book came from technical assistance reports written by Panasonic consultants listed in Appendix A; of particular usefulness were reports written by LaVaun Dennett, David Florio, Andrew Gelber, Patty Mitchell, Kenneth Tewel, and Earl Thomas. Several meetings with Sophie Sa and Ken Tewel also enhanced and clarified information in the book, as did a document prepared by Ruth Mitchell in 1994. Evaluation reports prepared by Education Resources Group's evaluation team were also extremely useful; team members included Ray del Portillo, Tonikiaa Orange, Jenny Ottinger, and Marcia Torres. Jacqueline Decker and Marian Watts prepared the manuscript. Kathleen Larson Florio edited the final draft of the manuscript.

Foreword

*T*he Panasonic Foundation's Partnership Program in school reform came about from a sense of frustration and not a small amount of naivete: frustration that the limited number and size of grants the foundation was able to make were not having a significant effect on the way this country's public schools operated—even those to which we made grants; and naivete about just how complex the issues were and how difficult it would be to achieve the ultimate result we were aiming for: better learning for every child.

The idea for what would become the Partnership Program was hatched one day when then foundation consultants Richard Lacey and Michael Holzman and I were sitting in my living room on the Upper West Side of Manhattan. We had just finished reading what seemed like hundreds of proposals for the third round of the foundation's school improvement grants. Although many of the proposed projects had merit, what impressed us most was how piecemeal and limited in scope they tended to be. One program would provide after-school tutoring to "at-risk" students; another would establish a summer institute on math and science for teachers; a third would train parents to help their children with reading; and so on.

Few proposals aimed at changing the school as a whole, and none addressed the systemic, district-level realities that in the long run make or break school-based initiatives. In addition, the proposals that came from schools, for the most part, did not seem to be acquainted with either the reform literature or reform efforts that were current at the time: Theodore Sizer's *Horace's Compromise* and Coalition of Essential Schools, the report of the Carnegie Forum on Education and the Economy, Phillip Schlechty's work, the efforts of the Central Park East schools in New York City, to name a few.

The consultants and I came to three conclusions: first, that more than money per se, schools needed ideas and knowledge; second, that school districts had to be part of the change effort; and third, that the change that was needed would take a long time to bring about: five years at a minimum, but probably closer to ten. We also felt that, rather than look for other agencies to work with schools and school districts, the foundation should provide technical assistance directly, through knowledgeable and experienced consultants we would identify. In other words, we would become, for all intents and purposes, an operating foundation rather than a grant-making one.

That was more than ten years ago. In the intervening years, the foundation has partnered with 16 school districts and 3 state departments of education. Our own assessment is that, for the most part, we have had a positive impact that in some cases has been major. And educators and others from the communities in which we have worked have concurred. State and district policies have changed so as to encourage greater autonomy and authority at the school site. Schools have redesigned their curricula, schedules, and assessment practices in order to improve the quality of learning for all children. Individual teachers and administrators feel more empowered. "Management" and "labor" are significantly more collaborative. There is a higher level of parent and community involvement in the schools.

At the same time, although less naive than we were at the beginning, we are in many ways as frustrated as ever with the two-steps-forward-one-step-back pattern of the reform efforts we've been involved with. No system we have partnered with has yet restructured to the degree we had hoped for. The number of good schools where we would send our own children is still in the minority. And we worry about the sustainability of those reforms we have helped put in place because resistance to change is such an integral part of the human condition, especially when the magnitude of the change that is needed is so great.

Nevertheless, we remain convinced that a systems approach focused on system-level restructuring, while not sufficient in and of itself, is absolutely necessary if enough of our schools are ever to get much better. And we continue to believe in the value of the technical assistance strategy, even as we strive to improve our technique and our results, in major part because our partners tell us how important it has been to have someone work alongside them as they daily face the daunting challenges of the change effort.

We have commissioned this book, then, not to demonstrate how "successful" the Panasonic Foundation has been. Proud as we are of the Partnership Program, we are a long way from declaring victory. Rather, it is to share our experiences and the insights we have gained in the hope that it will shed useful light on some of the issues that others engaged in similar efforts are also grappling with, and so contribute to the larger discourse about school reform. Naturally we would be thrilled if, in the course of reading this book, others are inspired to join the systemic reform cause or undertake our approach to technical assistance.

The authors are longtime associates of the foundation. Terry Clark is president of the Education Resources Group, which has provided a variety of valuable services to the foundation, including conducting a three-year evaluation of the Partnership Program. Richard Lacey, the foundation's very first consultant, was engaged originally to help in the reviewing of proposals in the area of elementary and secondary education and, as noted above, was instrumental in the development of the Partnership Program. Their deep knowledge of the foundation has enabled them to be both critics and friends who have called it as they have seen it in advising the foundation over the years, and in the writing of this book.

I would like to mention several other individuals, without whom there would not be a Partnership Program: the past and present members of the foundation's Board of Directors, collectively and individually, who, under the dedicated leadership of Chairman Robert Ingersoll, have been remarkably unwavering in their support of an approach that few, if any, other foundations have taken —one that cannot be touched, tasted, or "counted" and required an upfront commitment of at least ten years; the executives of Matsushita Electric, both in Japan and in the United States, who never once insisted that the foundation's programs be tied to either the corporation's business interests or its communities; and the senior consultants, especially Kenneth J. Tewel, whose knowledge and expertise are the heart of the Partnership Program, whose guidance I have relied upon at every step, and whose dedication to the enterprise tells me: we surely must be doing something right.

—Sophie Sa
Executive Director
Panasonic Foundation

The Panasonic Partnerships—An Overview

*T*he Panasonic Foundation created its Partnership Program for systemic educational reform in 1987 and has continued to develop it, steadily gaining knowledge, skill, and expertise. Panasonic believes the program's strength lies in its ability to raise questions and explore education reform issues. Its partnerships have attempted to open new avenues of inquiry within and among schools and school systems, encouraging entire communities to participate in decisions about children's learning.

The Panasonic Partnerships use technical assistance as a key strategy. What makes the strategy interesting is the intimate involvement of the foundation itself in helping to shape the reform process in partner districts through the use of expert, experienced consultants. This book seeks to encourage organizations and institutions involved in or considering work in public school reform to explore an approach in which external agents assist school systems to implement districtwide reform. It also provides schoolpeople with a third-party perspective on working within school systems on educational change.

Just as it presses school systems to question their educational traditions, structures, and practices, Panasonic has rigorously examined its own work, and its perspective on educational reform has evolved as a result of its close associations with school systems. After reflecting upon ten years of partnerships, the foundation has strengthened its resolve to engage school systems in the time-consuming, extraordinarily demanding process of fundamental

1

redesign. While the foundation believes it has learned a great deal and has useful insights about the art and science of stimulating, prodding, and supporting reform at the school district level, it is aware of how much learning remains to be done.

A Story Worth Telling

The Panasonic Partnerships story is worth telling for three reasons:

1. The Partnership Program is unique. No other philanthropic organization is known to have committed such substantial people resources rather than grant resources to a partnership concept focused on systemic reform: Panasonic has truly been a pioneer in this field. The foundation has also taken significant risks by making long-term commitments to support trial-and-error innovation in school systems: the Panasonic Partnerships have been subject to good and bad fortune and have withstood the unknowns that longitudinal commitments entail.

2. The program's basic concept and strategy are workable and ought to be refined, encouraged, and perhaps replicated. A focused, technical analysis of an emerging "Panasonic model" will help other philanthropies, technical assistance agencies, and school systems learn from the foundation's experiences.

3. These partnerships fascinate, for they combine art and science, knowledge and skill, intuition and analysis; they have revealed much about how governance policies and school board priorities affect teaching and learning. This book examines how the partnership strategy for systemic reform is played out in the context of school systems and their responses to change efforts.

Panasonic and Systemic School Reform

School systems are experiencing great stress, compounded by calls for accountability from politicians, business executives, and parent groups. The public demands that its schools "turn around" and "shape up," either by themselves or under new leadership or externally developed standards and mandates. Federal and state policies and "teacher-proof" approaches to education have consistently failed to improve educational achievement or to increase the number of students who benefit. Yet economic uncertainties, combined with intensifying social pressures, feed the American appetite for educational programs that promise to ensure basic student learning and achievement.

A diverse and growing body of research points to the need for an overhaul of America's public education systems. The research describes efforts around the country to change school systems and schools so that students have more equitable, appropriate, and updated opportunities for learning. Many of the change strategies and instructional innovations discussed in this book are products of these reform efforts and have been shown to be successful in improving teaching and learning processes. The reader may refer to this research for evidence that such strategies and innovations are worthy of adaptation and implementation in the quest for school improvement.

■

A diverse and growing body of research points to the need for an overhaul of America's public education systems.

Systemic school reform—transforming school systems in their entirety so that all children and youth are able to meet challenging learning standards—requires a sustained commitment, as well as know-how, and persistent collaborative effort. The Panasonic

Foundation commits its resources over a sufficient period of time to ensure three critical outcomes. First, all school constituencies must fully understand and accept proven school improvement concepts. Second, school systems and schools must integrate these concepts into their established practices and beliefs about teaching and learning, so that good schools are created and maintained. Finally, the improvement process must become part of the daily operations of school systems and schools.

The Panasonic Foundation's Mission, Beliefs, and Principles

Mission

The mission of the Panasonic Foundation is to help schools and school districts improve learning for all students so that they may use their minds well and become productive, responsible citizens.

Beliefs

All children can learn.

All students can achieve significantly higher levels of learning than they are currently achieving.

Principles

In order for all students to learn at higher levels, reform must aim at the whole school, and the school as a whole needs to be restructured.

State and local education systems must be restructured to support school-level reform.

Decisions affecting student learning must be made in a shared, participatory manner by those closest to the students, that is, by parents and the school staff.

Few schools, much less school systems, are organized or equipped for redesign, or "restructuring." Panasonic and its partners use this buzzword to refer to the redistribution of authority and responsibility within a school system. Rather than bureaucracy characterized by hierarchy and conformity, which experience has shown does not work, Panasonic's vision is of a system that is participatory, collegial, and focused on student success.

Authority and responsibility within a system are redistributed when leaders—superintendents and school boards, for example—facilitate rather than control staff efforts to create appropriate conditions for teaching and learning. As all participants learn new roles and behaviors, they work together to establish and adopt fresh expectations, goals, and objectives. Decision making about instructional practices takes place at the school level and includes teachers, who must have the requisite authority if they are willing to take responsibility.

The transition to this new type of governance structure at the district and school levels is stressful as well as liberating; threatening, confusing, and disruptive as well as empowering, focusing, and unifying. Resistance to institutional change is predictable and often formidable: it means unlearning old ways and learning new ways. Returning to old habits is natural, and the foundation has often had to remind its partners that the purpose of the partnership is to totally change the existing structure, not simply to repair it. Pursued collaboratively, the job of overcoming obstacles to systemic change may consume inordinate amounts of time, energy, and financial resources to achieve incremental gains.

The Foundation's Learning Process

The foundation's perspective on the nature and pace of significant and lasting school reform and the resources, conditions, and processes that lead to such reform has changed as it learned that the work is much harder and takes much longer than first imagined. Initially, Panasonic viewed school reform as a challenge to be addressed through mentorlike coaching. Increasingly, however, it has approached school reform more proactively, as foundation staff and consultants assume greater roles and responsibilities for ensuring the momentum of reform.

In 1985 the foundation formed a grant-making program in elementary and secondary school improvement, an initiative that resembled programs in other foundations at that time. For instance, grants supported projects to improve teaching and working conditions for teachers and to encourage increased community and

■

Resistance to institutional change is predictable and often formidable: it means unlearning old ways and learning new ways.

parental participation in school improvement. Within two years, however, the foundation staff and board determined that the program was yielding limited results because (1) American school systems tend to maintain outmoded structures, rules, decision-making processes, power relationships, and rewards; (2) school districts have a difficult time independently acquiring the necessary perspective and exercising the discipline to transform their schools; and (3) proposals submitted seldom addressed a whole school, much less an entire school system. The often narrow or shortsighted focus of these proposals and the disappointing results of many of those funded served to accentuate the daunting challenge of lasting systemic change.

The most promising ventures could not overcome the isolation experienced by even the more exemplary schools. Often the system in which an improving school was imbedded was not helping that school; sometimes the system harassed the school with central office demands for paperwork, time, and information; rarely did the central office attempt to learn from that school to facilitate improvements in other schools. Antediluvian patterns dominated the process used to make most educational decisions, macro and micro—from the size and cost categories of a metropolitan school district budget or the methods used to evaluate a child's learning to the number of minutes that a teacher has available to talk with colleagues during the school day.

Panasonic formed three conclusions: first, even more than funding, educators need to learn how to organize schooling differently; second, reform must occur at the school level, through teachers and administrators directly responsible for implementing improvements; and finally, systems themselves must be redesigned to support school-based reform. In 1987 Panasonic decided to redirect its funds toward systemic reform linked with whole-school restructuring.

An explicit principle for the Partnership Program, then, has been that the foundation forms partnerships with school districts, not with individual schools. Isolated school improvement is vulnerable and short-lived; it is rarely possible to improve schools in a lasting way unless the system changes over time to support and sustain the improvement. For lasting change to occur, the system itself must change—fundamentally and comprehensively—to provoke, facilitate, support, and nurture whole-school improvement.

Addressing Four Basic Needs

The foundation attempts to address four needs that it believes must be met if schools are to improve their capacity to educate all children and youth effectively.

First, educators need information and knowledge—*ideas*. In most cases these are gained through informal channels such as colleagues, and through formal settings such as workshops and seminars.

The Panasonic Foundation has worked with five states over the years of the Partnership Program. Foundation technical assistance has focused on helping state agencies change to support local schools and districts, and to align policies, goals, structures, and practices in support of challenging learning goals and opportunities for all students.

Much of the foundation's work with states has been an outgrowth of local partnerships. In two states, New Mexico and Minnesota, partnerships grew from efforts to engage state support for local partner districts— Santa Fe and Minneapolis. In New Jersey, the foundation worked with a state agency unit charged with helping urban districts. The unit, created by the Quality Education Act, was led by a former superintendent in a partner district. In recent years, the foundation has given targeted assistance to Rhode Island and Maine around learning standards and structures to support local districts, respectively.

The foundation's most active and longest relationship with a state is the ongoing partnership with New Mexico. The New Mexico Partnership began with a dialogue between the foundation, the State Department of Education, and the Santa Fe Public Schools. The partnership centers on the state's movement from a focus on ensuring regulatory compliance to providing support for local reform.

Among other activities, the foundation has conducted many department-wide retreats and reviews and has consulted with senior officials on ways to focus state support and guidance. An early product of the partnership was the state's "Invitation to Dream" initiative. This initiative asked local schools and districts to "think of the possibilities" if they were not limited by narrow rules, old habits, and a "gotcha" system of regulatory oversight. An initiative underway in 1996 is the "Education Plan for Student

Success." This initiative offers districts a new means of accreditation by the state and consolidates school and district planning in one comprehensive, systemic document.

Recognizing that state education policy and strategic direction are a product of several branches of government, the foundation has expanded its New Mexico Partnership to include the legislature and the governor's office. New Mexico is now engaged in strategic planning to develop a common vision and a comprehensive plan for education. This effort includes representatives of each branch of government; local education leaders; and business, community, and parental constituencies. The foundation facilitated the creation of legislation that, for the first time ever in New Mexico, includes all of these players in setting statewide educational policy.

Over the years, the New Mexico Partnership has led to changes in State Board of Education policy, a reorganization of department structure, department teams working across bureaucratic barriers, and an initiative to reduce needless reporting and the burdens of redundant application processes. The state has made progress in its efforts to support and guide local reform. While the state continues to play a monitoring and regulatory role, the culture of the department is moving toward a new supportive mode.

State government continues to be a resource for and potential barrier to reform. To the extent that the branches of state government work in harmony and provide local school systems with clear direction and a stable base of resources and encouragement, states are an important ingredient in local systemic reform.

Teachers inevitably seek new ideas and more information as they embark on school reform, but they tend to be isolated from colleagues in other schools and researchers in academia. Their thirst for new ideas can be met through exposure to other practitioners willing and able to share expertise and perspectives. Panasonic decided that an effective use of its resources would be to provide information and knowledge directly—primarily through sending in technical assistance consultants who are themselves educators.

■

Durable systemic reform is too complex to achieve in the short term, particularly in turbulent educational environments.

The second important need of educators is *training* in how to translate ideas into action. This can come from many sources: Panasonic imports expertise and special resources into a district to hold professional development seminars, institutes, and other forums for practitioner exchange. This is a cost-effective way to expose large numbers of school staff to new ideas and strategies, rather than relying on a few staff to take information back into the schools from outside the district. However, the foundation has also supported visits by practitioners to other school systems and training centers, and has sponsored periodic national roundtables and annual conferences for its partners.

The third need of educators engaged in the change process is for a *critical friend*, in Ralph Waldo Emerson's sense of the role: "Better be a nettle in the side of your friend than his echo." A critical friend can be a colleague who challenges, stimulates, and engages by raising important questions. Foundation consultants assume this role for superintendents and school board presidents, for schools and school communities, and, where possible, for teachers.

The fourth need of educators is for *close and enduring relationships*. The foundation has expended an extraordinary amount of effort building trust and credibility. Sustained engagement is essential for ensuring partners' confidence that the contract for change will endure for better or worse, and trust requires consistency of behavior based on an explicit and mutual set of values.

The foundation realized that durable systemic reform is too complex to achieve in the short term, particularly in turbulent educational environments. As many other school improvement efforts have demonstrated, an enlightened leader may leave unexpectedly; an exemplary program within a school may become isolated or embattled; a team of dedicated teachers may burn out or its members may assume new responsibilities or be transferred; and a shift in the political climate can devastate a school board or oust a superintendent. Only by staying for the long term can an external assister see a district through the turbulence and back to some degree of stability.

A Guide for Reading This Book

The foundation has commissioned this book in the hope that it may inform others interested in initiating, building, and maintaining systemic school reform. The book sets conceptual and strategic frameworks for collaborative reform, describes how Panasonic "makes" a partnership, highlights critical components such as technical assistance, and presents a series of vignettes and cases to illustrate how its approach has evolved over nearly a decade of school reform experiences.

The stories about Panasonic Partnerships included in this book are based on reports from the field written by the foundation's consultants; documentation reports submitted by the foundation's external evaluators; and a variety of documents from the districts, the schools, local media, and foundation leaders. Not all of the foundation's partnerships are discussed here; since the purpose is to be instructive about a strategy for systemic and whole-school reform, the processes described are in most cases more important than a particular partnership. And the lessons learned derive from the foundation's experiences across all of its partnerships, the elements of a change process evolving over time.

Chapter 1 describes how partnerships are initiated and formalized through a key "unleashing" event, usually focused on professional development. Technical assistance for systemic reform is described in Chapter 2 as the key component of the partnership strategy. Chapter 3 presents a case study of the first partnership, in Santa Fe, New Mexico. Other major components of the reform strategy, illustrating how systemic capacity to pursue change is built and sustained, are presented in Chapter 4. Chapter 5 includes a case study of a more recent partnership, with Allentown, Pennsylvania. The final chapter summarizes what the foundation has learned from its experiences and its evaluation study about the selection and nurturing of partnerships, critical factors in educational reform, and its enabling function in the reform process; and discusses plans for future partnerships.

Chapter 1

Partnership Building

San Diego, 1987

Panasonic senior staff remember the beginning this way:

> *A member of the San Diego Board of Education overheard a Panasonic program consultant discussing the Partnership Program during a meeting of the Council of Great City Schools... The board member suggested that superintendent Tom Payzant contact Panasonic's executive director, Sophie Sa. He did and they decided there was agreement between the District's and the Foundation's approach to systemic school-based reform.*

> —Holzman and Tewel, 1992

Former superintendent Tom Payzant remembers it this way:

> *I got involved by being at a meeting where Sophie Sa was talking to Richard Green, then superintendent in Minneapolis.... I tagged along to a luncheon, and I was intrigued by the conversation between the Minneapolis people and Sophie. That led to "why don't you come talk to us in San Diego?"*

> —Communication, 1995

Their stories agree that the initial contact happened by chance. Every step after that was purposeful.

The district and the foundation agreed to work together only after a series of exploratory meetings and introductory activities with teachers, administrators, and school board members. Discussions focused on the district's effort to begin a fundamental restructuring of schools, recommended by a blue-ribbon citizens commission in June 1987. An Innovation and Change Leadership Group composed of schoolpeople, board members, parents, and community representatives was organized to guide the restructuring initiative. The San Diego Teachers Association (SDTA) agreed in its new contract to work with the district to restructure schools, and the foundation offered consulting and technical assistance.

One district staff person later described Panasonic's role in those partnership-building days:

> The foundation was involved at every step. In the first stage it brought in teams to help us build knowledge about restructuring. In step two, when we had to make decisions, they had a couple of key workshops on "why restructure" and "how a team can go back and spread the gospel." This was a real motivator, having someone from the outside here saying, "you have the ingredients." We tried to bring the board along but sometimes found that we had shot ahead. We brought them into conferences to approve the policy on restructuring. So the foundation spent a lot of time with board members, which was key when we got into implementation. Panasonic asked good questions. This is very critical: you need someone from the outside to ask those questions. Also because Panasonic had a consortium of other sites, we knew that they had knowledge from other sites, and San Diego had the prestige of being part of a national effort.

By April 1988 the foundation was ready to sponsor an "unleashing event" to symbolize the now formal partnership status. San Diego's was a "Super Saturday," an orientation to the district's restructuring effort, attended by five-person teams from 38 of the 153 elementary and secondary schools. The foundation engaged a dozen practitioner-consultants from around the country to present a menu of reform ideas. Twenty-five schools participated in a follow-up "Super Planning Week," which involved intensive training in developing vision and mission statements, an implementation plan, and student and program assessment procedures. The San Diego Partnership had been launched.

Lancaster, 1994

Seeds for the Lancaster Partnership were sown in Panasonic's Allentown Partnership, when an Allentown administrator became the high school principal in nearby Lancaster. The Lancaster school district was implementing a five-year strategic plan, developed under state mandate, that emphasized "participatory management at all levels of the organization"; but this goal of school-based decision making (SBDM) had eluded district leadership. The high school principal thought that Panasonic's experience in this area could well be the perfect point of contact for the foundation and the district.

■

The goal of school-based decision making
had eluded district leadership.

He called a senior Panasonic consultant and also urged Lancaster's superintendent to contact the foundation about the Partnership Program. The first meeting between the foundation and the district took place at the end of April 1994. The consultant's three objectives were to inform district staff about the foundation's approach and activities; gauge their level of interest in working with the foundation; and learn about the district. He and another Panasonic consultant met with the superintendent; met over dinner with the superintendent's cabinet; had breakfast the next day with the current and past presidents of the teachers union; and visited the high school, a junior high school, and an elementary school.

■

Staff thought Panasonic's discussion raised provocative questions and forced them to think differently about how the schools were run.

Six weeks later Panasonic's executive director and several consultants visited Lancaster again to introduce the foundation to board of education members and meet a second time with union representatives and the superintendent's cabinet. The topic of these meetings was the status of the strategic plan implementation, focusing on curricular and organizational restructuring. Teachers knew that systemic reform and school-based reform were necessary, but reported that no one in the district knew how to restructure. Board members recognized the importance of the SBDM goal and that it was not yet being implemented, but did not want to become micromanagers. Staff thought Panasonic's discussion raised provocative questions and forced them to think differently about how the schools were run.

A recurring theme during these summer discussions was the district's preparedness for reform. The superintendent came to see through Panasonic's eyes that the buy-in to the reform "movement" in Lancaster was not as widespread as he had thought, and staff did not understand the definition of restructuring. Yet strong components of change were in place: a new high school building would open with the student body clustered into eight teams of 200 each; the junior high schools were being transformed into middle schools; the curriculum was being totally revised. Both the district and the foundation saw reasons to move forward.

Two major events had been planned by the end of August. A steering committee to lead reform was to meet in early November, and the Super Tuesday unleashing event was scheduled for the end of November. Panasonic had also met briefly with the Lancaster Alliance, a business group that had an eight-point agenda for the schools. It was important to align the belief systems of the foundation, the district, and the community.

The steering committee meeting went well: teachers were interested in participating in reform, and board members appeared committed to begin with school-based decision making. The consultant recommended that the partnership nurture relationships with "power centers" in the district, including the teachers union, the school board, and the superintendent's cabinet; and create a school-based coordinating group to start the reform process and to oversee its progress.

Fifteen hundred district and school employees participated in Super Tuesday, "On the Road to Site-Based Reform." They included instructional leaders and teachers, as well as classified personnel: food services staff, bus drivers, custodians, and clerical staff. Presenters were staff from reforming districts, including Panasonic's other partners. Cooperation and enthusiasm about the potential for change were widespread. Another partnership had been launched.

Critical Partnership Elements

These vignettes and the remainder of this chapter describe how the foundation selects and builds its partnerships upon critical themes: requiring commitment, asking questions, and nurturing constituencies.

Requiring Commitment

Willingness and commitment to change are the foremost criteria for becoming a partner district. Most partnership districts had at least some interesting ideas about restructuring or had begun a reform effort: San Diego was beginning a restructuring initiative; Lancaster was implementing key restructuring components, such as SBDM; Allentown was trying to implement an agreement with the teachers union that included school-based management. Panasonic wants to be absolutely sure, however, that a school system understands the meaning of partnership responsibilities, shares and is committed to the foundation's beliefs and goals, and is serious about restructuring the way it does business. The foundation determines if the district is willing to take these kinds of steps as evidence of district commitment to a partnership:

- reallocate human and financial resources to the schools to bring about reform;

- take risks to improve teaching and learning;

- examine the entire school system critically and support radical change;

- redefine district-school relationships, so that school-based reform is facilitated and supported by all players;

- commit to systemic, school-based reform as an ongoing way of life; and

- agree to a working relationship with the foundation for an extended period of time.

The foundation typically spends between six months and a year discussing, interacting, planning, and moving toward a key "unleashing" event with practitioners and school communities. In fact, there is no way to find out everything about a district at the outset: knowledge unfolds over time. The initial exploration and fact-finding conversations allow the two partners to agree that they have a congruity of purpose that supports starting a partnership.

Asking Questions

Many school practitioners who have benefited from partnership interactions have praised Panasonic for asking provocative questions. Typically, when a topic or area for reform is introduced, Panasonic consultants participate in a series of meetings with district and school staff to clarify definitions, expectations, and parameters for that aspect of reform.

Panasonic might ask the following questions about a district's infrastructure for developing professional and organizational capacity:

- Does the district provide high-quality, well-coordinated professional development?

- Do the school sites control resources for professional development and technical assistance?

- Are schools and teachers linked with networks and technologies within and beyond the district?

- Are business, education, and human service agency partnerships aligned with the district's strategic direction? Are they part of the infrastructure?

Panasonic might ask a different set of questions reflecting issues about transforming junior high schools into middle schools:

- Is there a general understanding of the middle school concept in the district?

- What are your reasons for preferring middle over junior high schools?

- What authority do you feel you have from the district to deal with the issue? To redesign schools?

- What are your hopes for interdisciplinary teams in middle schools?

- How do you see the middle school approach helping with discipline problems?

- Where are decisions about curricular and instructional changes made?

- How will you build teachers' capacity to implement a middle school philosophy?

- How do you know if the school works for the students? What are the indicators?

In general, foundation consultants ask questions but do not provide answers. They help the partner hypothesize and explore approaches to questions, or they ask questions that focus on the consequences of district policies and practices. "If site-based management is a stated district policy, why is the district still deciding which textbooks schools can use?" "When a student fails, who is held accountable? The student? The parents? The teachers? The district? For what are they held accountable, and how?"

Answers to such questions give the foundation information about problems in the school and the district, and they also begin to give schoolpeople perspective on their difficulties and the impetus to explore further. When a consultant asks, for example, "What authority has the district given you as a school to redesign the school?" the teachers and principal ask themselves if they have the support they need. Are they really able to make decisions at the site? Will their decisions be respected at the central office, or overridden?

Meanwhile, the district formulates its own questions and contacts other partnership districts to get information. Is the foundation's belief system about reform aligned with ours? Is the foundation

■

All the questions tend toward one master question for the district:
Are we as a school system ready to form
a partnership with an outside group?

imposing its own agenda on us? Will it cause turmoil we don't want? What will we get from the partnership? Since the district will not receive a grant, what is the extent of foundation support for staff development and other kinds of activities? What does that support look like? These questions must be considered as the foundation and the district size each other up. All the questions tend toward one master question for the district: *Are we as a school system ready to form a partnership with an outside group, the Panasonic Foundation, to rethink our approach to educating students and managing the system?*

This critical question is answered differently by various players in the district, especially if some tension already exists among them. A superintendent, for example, may want to push change along rapidly. A high-level administrator may have decided that SBDM will interfere with the ability to continue working the same way as in the past and may seek to undermine any moves in that direction.

A cabinet member who heavily influenced the reform agenda may see the foundation as another pair of hands for his reform. A board member may be most concerned about losing control of the district to an outside party.

Nurturing Constituencies

Foundation representatives display a blend of behaviors when building a partnership: speech making, salesmanship, coaxing, information sharing, and parameter setting. With each potential partner, they develop a strategy for nurturing constituencies based on the status of the school system's reform efforts and the particular areas in which innovations are being attempted.

■

A partnership with the foundation is not necessarily welcomed by all constituencies in a school system. As an outsider, Panasonic has been perceived as having a hidden agenda.

During this process, foundation consultants are sensitive to a district's desire to adhere to its own agenda. Often a superintendent has invited the foundation in recognition of a need for assistance in implementing a major reform effort. In Lancaster, for example, the superintendent acknowledged early on that he needed more help than he had originally thought in structuring a reform process and nurturing endorsement from his staff and faculty.

A partnership with the foundation is not necessarily welcomed by all constituencies in a school system. As an outsider, Panasonic has been perceived as having a hidden agenda. One district staff person put it this way:

Panasonic came in under the umbrella of "facilitator" to assist us in moving in this direction. Now they are viewed as an organization with a "bag of tricks" or their own program which they are encouraging us to implement.

The foundation has also been criticized for having a rigid educational philosophy, discouraging activities that do not conform to this philosophy, and declining to sponsor activities it does not advocate. In fact, Panasonic considers requests for assistance in terms of how they contribute to restructuring. It considers the merits of a specific request within the framework of reform goals established mutually by the partners. When this basic distinction is not fully understood and school partners feel like supplicants, staff frustration leads to conflict. The foundation learned from this that commitment to collaboration with a school district entails building and rebuilding trust, and periodically renegotiating the terms of the partnership.

What the foundation supports is based on an understanding of best practices derived from experience and research about their effectiveness. Panasonic's push for the use of authentic assessments, for example, is attractive to partners who are ready to explore and pilot alternatives to conventional, standardized approaches to measuring student learning. Even districts most enthusiastic about authentic assessment recognize, however, that standardized tests are more accepted, easier to administer, and less expensive. As one Minneapolis district leader explained, Panasonic continues to oppose standardized tests, yet the school board there insists on timely, comprehensive, understandable (to them) accountability data, and tests offer the obvious, readily available measures. He feels that the foundation "places more emphasis on being right than on getting people where they need to be."

Sometimes resentments build among different role groups in partner districts:

> *Panasonic supports reform among the teachers, but closes its eyes to what the administrators are doing.*
>
> —Teacher (quoted in *Education Week*, 1994)

I think the foundation should spend more time talking with district leadership about what they have to offer and the change process. They should meet with principals and those interested in restructuring about what it is and the implications so principals can prepare their schools for the consultants. The principals were ignorant on what the consultants could do. Some joined their staff in expressing hostility. I would implore the superintendent to make sure that key members of the staff were very well versed on what the Panasonic Foundation was into and going to do so they could move full speed.... I would not wait as long as we did to have a retreat for district staff and principals.

—District staff person

Most feedback about Panasonic's approach to nurturing reform is positive, however, and centers on the foundation's desire to broaden educators' vision and provide otherwise scarce resources. One staff development leader said the foundation "is a great stimulus for the district. It comes in and prods us, and we react." Comments from staff and community players in Allentown also reflect Panasonic's catalytic role in forging partnerships:

Panasonic has been the driving force and impetus for change.

The summer workshops and increased parent involvement were particularly helpful outcomes of Panasonic's involvement.

Panasonic's involvement has empowered teachers and given them a new sense of professionalism.

Minneapolis's superintendent gave the district's partnership high marks in early 1995 for building support for reform among school board members and union representatives. Foundation consultants who facilitate board retreats have gotten particularly good reviews. Following are examples of how Panasonic worked with the Lancaster Board of Education on its mission to "transform itself" and with the teachers union in San Diego.

Working with a Board

The Lancaster Board of Education met with Panasonic at a November 1994 retreat on "Levels of Board Work." The outcome of that session was a framework for how the board would allocate its time during three hours per week of meetings. The board would devote half of its time to "long-term strategies to achieve the district's vision"; about 30 percent to policy and budget development; and about 10 percent to each of two activities—making immediate administrative decisions and ceremony.

With assistance from a Panasonic consultant at a February 1995 retreat, the board identified key issues and strategies for addressing issues, and chose two focus areas:

1. How can we improve results for 100 percent of students so that all will be ready for work and further education?

2. How can we increase and broaden community allies to meet our goal in focus area #1?

The group addressed a strategy for enlisting community allies at an August 1995 retreat, where the consultant became an observer and commentator rather than a facilitator. The group outlined concerns and issues about the Lancaster community's relationship to the district and discussed strategies for nurturing it. Excerpts from the consultant's written notes to the board after that retreat are informative:

Congratulations on doing what you have been wanting to do as a board. You made the commitment to have a different approach to work sessions, one that would permit "real discussion" and include other stakeholders.... You talked about your concept of an effective board as one that spends much of its time on major problems and serves as the interface between the community and the school system. Many boards talk about this, but find that changing the way they operate is difficult. You should be commended for transforming the way you work to support the changes you want to see among district and school staff.

Working with a Teachers Union

The foundation has made it a point to work extensively with teachers union representatives, because engaging them while building a partnership is essential. Its 1993 Partnership Conference theme, for example, was unions as leaders in reform. Its work with the teachers union in San Diego illustrates its purpose.

The leader of the San Diego Teachers Association (SDTA) had been personally involved with the superintendent's team during the early San Diego Partnership days. Under a new superintendent and new union leadership in 1993, however, communications were not as good. Relations worsened later that year, when the school board passed a resolution directing the district to reassign teacher-certified personnel who were not teaching back into regular classrooms to reduce class size and the number of district staff. The union represented persons who would be affected by the resolution—counselors and nurses, for example—and administrators, not teachers, would be making decisions about the reassigned staff lines and functions.

■

Teachers viewed the state's charter school movement and the district's exploration into privatized school management as substantial threats.

The SDTA itself was in need of rejuvenation. Its members had not received a pay raise in four years, and teachers viewed the state's charter school movement and the district's exploration into privatized school management as substantial threats. The African-American community was accusing teachers of being racist, and internal challenges from the SDTA's own members were becoming more frequent.

Prior union leadership had cooperated with and supported the district's reform efforts. *Education Week* reported in 1989 that the SDTA was "probably the largest affiliate of the NEA to provide such unqualified support for a restructuring initiative." It quoted the union president: "Now's the time when whoever takes the initiative in restructuring is going to be in control." Five years later, despite the union's cooperation and support, most schools still lacked capacity to competently implement school-based change efforts.

∎

The union, having cast its lot with reform,
was demanding contract clauses that specifically addressed
components of the restructuring initiative.

Panasonic saw an opportunity to help the union take a leadership role in reform: support for "union transformation and capacity building" became one of three key areas for Panasonic involvement in San Diego's systemic reform movement. A foundation consultant worked with union members to arrange a symposium focused on exhibiting teacher leadership in reform and nurturing teachers' relationships with an increasingly vocal community.

The consultant and the union planned the retreat for November 1994 to promote conversation among union leaders from several restructuring districts on issues of leadership, frameworks for reform, and waivers. This meeting in San Diego of union leaders from Allentown, Boston, Dade County, Louisville, and Minneapolis included SDTA leaders from a third of San Diego's schools. It represented a proactive approach to union leadership in systemic reform.

Union/partnership interactions slowed when contract negotiations between the board and the union began in 1995. District staff still commended Panasonic for facilitating communications. The SDTA was working actively, for example, with the district's staff development director on implementation of the Rockefeller Foundation's school reform initiative, "Building an Infrastructure for Professional Development." And the union, having cast its lot with reform, was demanding contract clauses that specifically addressed components of the restructuring initiative and would guarantee district follow-through.

Building Future Partnerships

Panasonic intends to apply the insights gained in early partnerships to promote restructuring in additional public school districts. The critical themes discussed in this chapter—requiring commitment, asking questions, and nurturing constituencies—will be important criteria for engagement in new partnerships. They are summarized here.

- Willingness and commitment to change are the foremost criteria for becoming a partner district. The exploration period before a partnership is established allows both parties to agree on purpose, commit to partnership beliefs and goals, understand partnership responsibilities, and confirm a serious intent to work together toward restructuring schools.

- The exploration period is highlighted by a series of conversations between the district and the foundation, during which both information-gathering and thought-provoking questions are raised. The purpose of asking questions is to clarify definitions, expectations, and parameters of the anticipated reform effort.

- As the foundation builds a partnership, it develops a strategy for nurturing important constituencies who will participate in the reform effort. Foundation consultants work closely with school boards, central office and school staff, union leaders, and the community to ensure that knowledge, understanding, and trust guide partnership activities.

Chapter 2

Technical Assistance as a Strategy for Systemic Reform

- *It's Super Tuesday in Lancaster. Schools are closed and all staff are attending workshops on school reform strategies conducted by Panasonic consultants from around the country. The consultants will later facilitate staff teams as they select strategies for their own schools: alternative methods of student assessment; multiage student grouping; site-based management; increasing parent involvement; and thematic instruction.*

- *A Panasonic-sponsored conference in Minneapolis focuses on redesign of the district's student assessment system to ensure higher quality and more diverse data on academic progress. The superintendent, board members, and school and district staff draft a "strategic direction" for student assessment.*

- *A school team prepares a presentation to the Santa Fe Board of Education on an innovation the school wants to implement. A Panasonic consultant helps the team apply for a State Education Department waiver so the innovation can be implemented.*

- *Panasonic consultants hold a three-day workshop for a Minneapolis high school staff on "Empowering Students and Human Relations." The school then develops a six-week instructional unit on the topic for ninth-graders.*

- *At a foundation-sponsored school retreat in Santa Fe, principals and teachers are in disagreement over plans for site-based management. The Panasonic facilitator arranges for a local mediator at the group's request, and they are able to develop shared decision-making guidelines.*

- *A Panasonic consultant facilitates a retreat for the Lancaster Board of Education to make key decisions about its levels of work, focus areas, and principles and procedures.*

- *Allentown's Leadership Alliance—a local network of businesses and community groups organized to support the district's reform process—evolves from meetings of the superintendent and the Panasonic and Rider-Pool Foundations.*

- *A dinner meeting to plan a symposium for the San Diego teachers union highlights presentations to be given by union members from other partnership districts who have provided leadership in school reform.*

- *The first meeting of Parent Teacher Association leaders from seven San Diego schools that make up a "cluster" is facilitated by a Panasonic consultant, who helps them plan ways to work together, coordinate support efforts, and promote community relationships.*

These illustrations portray diverse, ongoing technical assistance that Panasonic provides to develop practitioners' capacities for discovering and using innovative educational strategies. The foundation emphasizes ideas and training on how to translate ideas into action for systemic reform. *This strategy has been key to Panasonic's approach to systemic change.*

The Role of Technical Assistance

Panasonic's role as long-term partner began with its initial partnership in Santa Fe, New Mexico, where the foundation sponsored workshops, direct consultation, and visits to other schools and school systems to acquaint teachers, administrators, parents, school board members, and central office staff with ideas and practices that could improve education in the district. The objective was to help teachers and administrators define and pursue a radically different direction in their professional lives in response to new expectations and opportunities.

■

The Panasonic technical assistance strategy emphasizes
how to translate ideas into action for reform.

This focus on professional development led Panasonic to establish a cadre of technical assistance consultants who would take activist roles in provoking, supporting, and sustaining educational change. The role of the Panasonic consultant is to actively help people rethink how educational roles and responsibilities are performed throughout a school system.

Panasonic's consultants are committed to system-level change, realizing that schools are affected—and often limited—by the larger policy and budgetary contexts in which they operate. At the same time, their work with individual schools assumes that change efforts affect student learning only if they are led by those directly responsible for teaching and learning. Consultants therefore link the larger vision of systemic reform to concrete operational details in schools and classrooms.

Consultants introduce ideas, train, and encourage problem solving and reflection. They observe district and school staff assess their needs and plan for improvement. They meet with superintendents, leadership teams, grade-level teams, academic departments, special services personnel, whole school faculties, cross-campus groups, central office staff, principals association and union leaders, school boards, community and parent groups, business leaders, and any other group that is or should be part of the district restructuring and school reform processes. They plan and participate in events, and they are available afterward for on-site follow-up. And they are in constant phone communication with the district.

Consultants equip district personnel to stretch and build their capacities to conceive, plan, and develop worthwhile school improvement programs. Consultants stimulate thinking and expand participants' conceptions of their own capabilities and opportunities. No other feature of the foundation's approach to school reform elicits as many comments as the effects of consultants on local capacity.

> *Panasonic shares its information with staff and encourages them to experiment with new ideas and approaches.*

> *Foundation consultants help teachers by answering their questions and stimulating thinking.*

> *Foundation representatives serve as provocateurs, as well as providers of support.*

> *They offer a reflective critique; their role is key to prodding and pushing us forward.*

> *They didn't give us the recipe, but referred us to people. We're making our own recipe now.*

> *Panasonic brought people in long enough for us to get to know them. This people linkage is important.*

> *We are learning to be resources to each other, learning to learn.*

Who Is a Panasonic Consultant?

The foundation provides technical assistance to its partners through a network of more than 200 consultants. Most of the consultants are practicing teachers and administrators—sometimes discovered in partnership sites. Among the 200, a core of 15 to 20 senior consultants have a long-term and close working relationship with the foundation. Some senior consultants work with schools and districts on an ongoing basis to facilitate and participate in partnership development. Others serve as expert resources on particular topics. They also tend to fill a variety of other roles for the foundation, including providing advice and counsel about the Partnership Program.

The foundation's senior consultants constitute a widespread network that is connected to education reform efforts around the country. They tend to be expert, seasoned educators who have initiated or facilitated systemic education reform, school restructuring, and instructional improvement. They are recognized for their experience in working with district officials and school staffs and their ability to support and sustain improvement efforts. They are identified through word of mouth, recommendations via the nationwide professional network, a reputation for excelling in their own districts in school reform efforts, or requests by partnership districts for specific staff development events.

Candidates for consultancies are carefully selected: their backgrounds in education must include successful, relevant experience and evidence of the interpersonal skills needed to work with schoolpeople as a true partner. They must be capable of developing relationships and engaging in dialogue, respectful of others' fears and concerns, skilled at facilitating and questioning, and able to encourage, motivate, inspire, and garner commitment to change.

The senior consultants' credibility with partners leads to two important outcomes: (1) relationships develop between Panasonic consultants and district educators that allow open communication and meaningful work to take place; and (2) assistance goes well beyond traditional training and knowledge transfer, as the consultant is available to help with implementation issues, the deepening of knowledge, and the development of local capacity for self-help.

A Diversity of Topics

A listing of the topics covered by foundation consultants as they have provided training in process skills and helped school staffs implement educational reform would exceed the syllabi of most professional development centers. Topics are determined both by the sites and the foundation and depend on where a district sits along the reform continuum. The following are representative:

- *Governance:* school-based decision making; new roles for school boards and central office personnel; management.

- *School restructuring:* alternative scheduling; heterogeneous and multiage student grouping; organizing students and teachers into families or teams; team teaching; restructuring the school day for teacher planning.

- *Curriculum:* integrated curriculum; development of thematic units; varieties of instructional materials (beyond textbooks); reading, writing, and whole language; mathematics, science, and technology.

- *Instruction:* cooperative learning; holistic teaching; hands-on learning; use of technology; use of the Socratic method.

- *Student assessment:* alternative methods of assessment; use of portfolios and exhibitions; progress reporting to parents.

- *Students and student learning:* early childhood education; developmentally appropriate programs and instruction; early adolescence; student empowerment.

- *Community relations:* school relationships with family, community, and business.

A Diversity of Forums

Forums for staff development are typically workshops—ranging from one day to two weeks—and retreats for school staffs, job-alike groups from across the district (e.g., secondary principals, Title I coordinators, special education teachers), central office personnel, school board members, school and district leadership teams (which often include parents), and union leadership teams. Participants share a common focus or are working toward a common goal. For example, they may be teachers who will be developing new curricula, implementing new teaching strategies, and using new methods of assessing student learning; principals with new roles in schools managed by leadership teams using shared decision-making strategies; or leadership teams who will be developing and managing site-based budgets and implementing new schedules and student grouping patterns.

Panasonic also sponsors larger gatherings with participants from several or all partnership districts, and focused "roundtable" conferences that address specialized topics for ad hoc district teams.

A fall 1994 Restructuring Roundtable sponsored by Panasonic and the Allentown Education Association defined the role of technology in systemic restructuring; its objectives were to (1) assist districts and states in developing guiding principles and planning processes for technology and (2) establish an ongoing, cross-district technology support group. The status of technology use in eight school districts and three states was featured, as were demonstrations and discussions about integrating instructional technology with communications, application, and curriculum.

The foundation also uses site visits to other districts and schools as mechanisms to expose staff to new ideas and methods. While Turquoise Trail Elementary School in Santa Fe and O'Farrell Community School in San Diego were being planned, for example, the foundation sponsored visits by teams from both districts to the Central Park East schools in New York City, known for their progressive instructional approaches. Visiting sites where new practices have been implemented allows teachers and principals to observe innovative strategies in action and in settings similar to their own. These visits give credibility to both presenters and ideas. And they give educators an opportunity to ask questions of fellow practitioners.

Benefits to Partners

Access to Information

Superintendents, principals, and teachers value Panasonic for its national perspective and access to a rich information and knowledge base.

> *Panasonic helps district staff to know what site-based management looks like and how to do it. They give guidelines and examples, places to call and contact.*

> *They offer us a broader perspective, tell us about other districts.*

> *The foundation's resources have provided the expert guidance needed to make informed decisions about the best approaches to school improvement.*

> *What Panasonic is doing is allowing them [school staffs] to open up to ideas that the district had never thought of before.*

The networking that occurs among Panasonic partners is invaluable and is a rich component of the overall reform approach supported by the foundation.

Improved Communications

Partnership activities help to improve communications within school buildings and across districts. Restructuring events give school professionals a focus for conversation. Following workshops on restructuring in Minneapolis, for example, district leaders created the "Five with Five" group, made up of five representatives from the teachers union and five from the Principals' Forum, to continue discussing restructuring issues. Initial Allentown training sessions led to a coordinating group that focused on planning.

Panasonic helped us get school councils, and school councils brought more communication to the school.

The greatest impact Panasonic has made seems to be on communication among staff for decision making and planning.

Panasonic was involved in clarifying channels of communication.

The partnership has pulled staff together to discuss sharing the same teaching philosophy and to support each other.

Panasonic involvement has been crucial in helping staff become more articulate.

Climate for Change and Risk Taking

Partnership districts are more open to innovation.

Panasonic helped the school by setting a climate in the district that supported innovation and encouraged people to do different things.

Panasonic made it easier for teachers who wanted to do things
by setting the stage for risk takers ... and for schools to have
their own personality.

Working with teachers and principals on restructuring and
improving instruction, Panasonic consultants have helped develop structures for problem solving and have helped solve specific
problems that might otherwise obstruct change or discourage risk
taking. A superintendent stated, "There is clear evidence that
schools are learning to problem solve and explore flexibility in
approaches."

Because the foundation works with central office administrators as
well, it has demonstrated that problems between districts and
schools can be solved. One principal said, "Panasonic provided a
link and sometimes ran interference on behalf of the school at district offices."

Staff Empowerment

A basic premise of the Partnership Program is that teachers need to
be treated as and view themselves as professionals. Employees
who are in control of their working conditions and participate in
making decisions not only are happier but are more likely to take
responsibility for their work. A number of teachers in partnership
districts are now directly contacting national experts, as well as
their superintendent and state education department leaders, with
questions and comments; before, because they were "just teachers," they would not have dared do this. Repeatedly, teachers and
administrators speak of their own sense of empowerment and the
energy that derives from this.

The most valuable thing about the Panasonic consultants is how
they have empowered staff and individual teachers and princi-
pals to develop and implement new ideas for instruction.

Panasonic is empowering teachers by believing in the value of what they have to say.

Panasonic gave us the "guts" to go for this.

Panasonic put the fire back into my commitment to education.

Panasonic allowed teachers to recognize their own areas of expertise.

With support and technical assistance, new knowledge, a developing climate for change, renewed vigor, and a sense of professionalism, partnership schools and districts are actively engaged in the slow and arduous process of educational reform. Students are working more in collaborative groups and on integrated curriculum projects. Teachers are basing their instruction on an understanding of the variety of student learning styles. Districts are measuring student progress through different methods of assessment, rather than an exclusive reliance on paper-and-pencil testing. School decision-making teams are replacing traditional authority structures, with parents and teachers joining administrators in making decisions. New daily schedules are allowing more flexibility to accommodate different instructional needs and provide planning and meeting time for teachers. New ways of organizing district offices—including new roles and responsibilities for central office staff members—are emerging, as are new ways of maintaining communication between the central office and the individual school sites.

School board members, superintendents, central office staff, principals, teachers, and parents credit the Panasonic Partnership Program both for the support it provides and for the way it goes about its work. One superintendent summarized the special characteristics of Panasonic's nontraditional technical assistance approach by

The O'Farrell Way

Development of the O'Farrell Community School was an opportunity seized: the San Diego Unified School District had growing enrollment, an empty building, and a state climate for middle school reform. A planning team of central office leaders and the teachers association spent two years envisioning concepts and themes for the new middle school, greatly assisted by the Stuart and Panasonic Foundations.

The Stuart Foundation provided resources for a week-long planning session in August 1989 for newly appointed team members ..., planning retreats, and major trips for team members to other innovative school programs ... The Panasonic Foundation served as a resource to the San Diego City Schools' efforts by linking the district to teachers, administrators, and educational consultants involved in planning and implementing educational change efforts nationwide. [It has] been influential in the initial planning sessions for the team over the last year.*

One team of Panasonic-sponsored consultants came from Capshaw Middle School in Santa Fe (a partnership district). Capshaw's structure was similar to that proposed for O'Farrell, and its team shared knowledge and exper-

citing its hands-on nature, its commitment and involvement, and its emphasis on learning from change. His observation highlights the dual nature of the partnership relationship:

> *You have both an internal and an external relationship that increases your credibility with staff and gives a sense that we are in this together rather than being watched from afar.*

It is this sense of being in it together rather than being watched from afar that makes the Panasonic Partnership Program and the technical assistance it provides so meaningful and potentially effective.

tise during a March 1990 weekend retreat on governance and structure for the O'Farrell planning group. Panasonic's role in this process was to facilitate collaborative planning and collegial sharing and support through provision of expert resources and information about innovative practices.

O'Farrell Community School opened in September 1990, structured around educational "families" of 150 students and 6 teachers each. Students are expected to complete an eighth-grade project with oral, written, and visual components and present a "portfolio" of work that documents academic, social, and emotional growth.

Reflection and assessment are integrated into school life. Teachers have daily common preparation periods to plan curriculum and discuss issues, and staff retreats are held to share concerns and solve problems. A Community Council consisting of school staff, parents, and students makes all decisions concerning schoolwide operations, enhancing an overall sense of ownership in the school.

---

* From *Restructuring: An Inside Look*, by P. Goren and K. Bachofer, San Diego Unified School District, June 1990, p. 7.

Annual Partnership Conferences and Roundtables

The Panasonic Foundation has sponsored annual partnershipwide conferences to serve several purposes:

- providing key stakeholders from each partnership district uninterrupted time to work as a team and address in some depth issues of critical importance;
- renewing individual and collective commitment to the systemic reform process;
- encouraging cross-district sharing and support; and
- developing "communities of interest" across partnership districts and reminding districts that they are part of a larger reform community.

The foundation works closely with district staff to match the conference agenda with the districts' needs and priorities. Growing participation in the two-and-a-half-day events—teams from participating districts have increased in size from about 8 members to about 15—along with specific feedback, indicates that districts find the conferences to be increasingly relevant and useful to their endeavors.

Conference topics include the following:

1989 Assessment in the Service of System-Level and Systemic Restructuring

1990 Assessment, Equity, and Accountability in the Context of Systemic, School-Based Reform

1991 Learning Outcomes and Accountability in the Context of Systemic, School-Based Reform

1992 School Board and Central Office Leadership in a Time of Fiscal Austerity: How to Sustain Systemic, School-Based Restructuring

1994 A New Social Compact: Lasting Partnerships for Reform Among the School Board, Central Office, and Teachers Union

1995 Closing the Gap: Every Student a Learner, Every School a Success

1996 Communicating Change Internally and Externally to Sustain Systemic Reform

The 1996 conference addressed the need to improve communications internally—within the school district—and externally—positively engaging the public. The messages of several conference speakers were later distilled into the following five principles of effective communications:

1. Keep the message simple and repeat it often.
2. Keep the message consistent, remembering that communication is much more than speeches and official documents.
3. Involve various stakeholder groups in creating and delivering the message and pay particular attention to teachers and parents.
4. It's at least as important to listen as it is to talk.
5. Address your message to people's bottom-line concern: "What's in it for me (or my child)?" but also appeal to "the better angels of their nature"—that is, their civic and community spirit.

Much of the conference was devoted to working sessions that provided an opportunity for teams to connect the ideas and insights raised by speakers with the realities in their particular district. The Broward County (Florida) Public Schools team, for example, recognized that one of its biggest challenges was hooking in the 80 percent of district residents who have no children in the schools.

The team received guidance during the conference from representatives of the Edmonds (Washington) School District. One observation that clicked was the statement that "buy-in from the participants is critical." The team came to realize that most past communication strategies in the district had sought participation too late in the process. They resolved to develop an action plan to "take the pulse" of the community and begin implementation.

Over the next five months, working independently and with a Panasonic consultant, the district developed a two-phase process for communicating

(continued on page 46)

major district and school initiatives—a process that directly involves key stakeholders. They called the process "The Communication Loop."

Beginning in January 1994, district teams have also joined together for smaller-scale "Restructuring Roundtables." Topics have been "Strategies for Creating Collaboratives to Insure Integration and Coordination of Reform Initiatives" (January 1994), "Technology to Support, Sustain, and Deepen Systemic Restructuring" (October 1994 and October 1995), and "School Clustering as a Strategy for Systemic Restructuring" (November 1996).

Chapter 3

Santa Fe, New Mexico—
Origins of the Partnership Concept

*T*he Partnership Program originally developed from the premise that an enlightened and energetic superintendent would welcome working closely with a partner committed to providing resources to improve the system and its schools over several years. The foundation envisioned numerous ways of working with a school system to support improvement efforts designed and managed by the schools themselves. Supported both informally and publicly by the superintendent, the foundation could reinforce district leadership by working directly with any and all schools that wanted its help.

Administrative components, especially the central office, would change in response to downward pressure from the superintendent, upward pressure from individual schools, external pressure, and encouragement and resources from the foundation. Over time, the maturing partnership would focus the activities and concerns of the school community at every level on substantially improving the quality of teaching and learning in schools districtwide, and the partnership's efforts would be reflected in high levels of achievement for all students.

Benefiting from experience with subsequent partner districts, Panasonic gradually revised its original strategy for educational reform. The foundation realized that it lacked the resources—both people and funds—necessary to work effectively with all schools in a district, especially when the majority of them are distressed schools with long-term needs. But even more fundamental, Panasonic learned that its intensive involvement at the system level, including working directly with the central office, was critically important to educational reform.

The Original Vision for Change

The Santa Fe Partnership was the foundation's first attempt to apply its school-based, whole-school reform strategy. It offered an exciting prospect: school reform would be led by teachers and facilitated by an array of expert practitioner-consultants. The foundation would assume a highly visible, active role—monitoring progress, advising school leaders, suggesting alternatives, convening participants, analyzing options, questioning choices, and responding to direct requests for assistance.

The foundation hypothesized that initial opposition to change might last as long as a year or more in light of local culture. Many senior teachers, for example, were bound to resist rapid change. As one school board member explained, some teachers who had taught in the same classroom 15 years or more had become accustomed to their routines: "They drive up to their parking lot, they walk to their classroom, they teach their class, they walk back to their vehicle, and they're gone.... They're comfortable. Change is threatening."

Despite this attitude, foundation staff and senior consultants concurred that visible endorsement of school reform from the superintendent, together with political support by the school board, should gradually overcome the barriers. The vision driving the foundation was its belief that pockets of resistance would be chipped away by (1) appropriate conditions over time, (2) momentum for school-based reform, (3) sustained support from the top, (4) instructional practices that had been successful elsewhere, and (5) clear evidence of improved teaching and learning in a restructuring school. After five or more years of immersion in the restructuring process, school and district leaders and staff would become accustomed to thoughtful educational management and would share a common vision of high expectations for students' educational performance. Collectively they would build the capacity of local schools to enable all students to achieve at high levels.

■

The Santa Fe Partnership offered an exciting prospect:
school reform would be led by teachers
and facilitated by an array of expert practitioner-consultants.

The foundation thought that teachers, rather than superintendents or outstanding principals, should occupy center stage, because they are closer to students. Assisted by expert consultants and taking part in activities funded by the foundation, teachers would identify needs and set goals, critically examining their practices and gaining exposure to other ways of teaching and learning. They would become "empowered."

This expanding awareness, coupled with heightened expectations, would increase the pressure for deep restructuring and teacher-led, school-based decision making. These would ultimately result in changes in instructional practice and in the overall school district culture.

A Challenge to Long-Term Reform

Many of the techniques that now characterize the Panasonic Partnerships were forged in Santa Fe, as the foundation worked with Superintendent Edward Ortiz to improve the quality of education in local schools. The challenge of redefining a long-term partnership after Mr. Ortiz's sudden death in 1991 tested whether systemic change—however well nourished by the past administration—could survive a change in top leadership.

Mr. Ortiz's death forced the foundation to examine its strategy for reform in light of the notoriously high turnover among superintendents and the political volatility of school boards across the country. The experience also helped Panasonic understand the need for helping school boards and their communities clarify a vision, develop a sense of where the district must be headed, and determine the kind of superintendent it should hire based on its vision and direction. In the laboratory of the Santa Fe Partnership, the foundation realized the importance of helping to create optimal conditions for selecting leaders for educational reform. This perspective later guided the foundation's work in other districts, where it has provided resources and support for selecting new superintendents.

The duration of the Santa Fe Partnership (1987–95), the dramatic positive and negative changes that occurred over time, and the early absence of other partnerships competing for attention gave the foundation the opportunity—and at times forced it—to reexamine its assumptions, beliefs, and practices. By remaining faithful to a cornerstone principle of its original (but untested) concept of long-term commitment, the foundation explored many critical questions and issues and developed techniques that guided its initiatives elsewhere. Equally important, the Santa Fe Partnership enabled the foundation to develop a deeper appreciation for the complex nature of comprehensive reform in school districts and the role of an outside partner.

Origin of the Santa Fe Partnership

The Santa Fe public school system serves 12,500 students in 25 schools. The population of the school district is about half Hispanic, with a higher percentage in the elementary schools. Less than 2 percent of the students are Native American. Since 1987 the district has opened new schools, largely to accommodate the burgeoning Hispanic population, the result of both birthrate and in-migration. One of the 4 middle schools opened in fall 1994, and 1 of the 18 elementary schools, Turquoise Trail, was developed with a great deal of assistance from the partnership.

Foundation staff visited Santa Fe in March 1987 at the invitation of the newly installed president of St. John's College, who wanted to reach out to the community by attracting foundation funds to support school improvement activities. In preparation, Superintendent Ortiz issued a memo to all employees asking for ideas on an improvement plan. His memo urged teachers to "think big" about how to bring about real change in the schools. Like Panasonic, he believed strongly in teacher empowerment and local planning as strategies for accomplishing reform.

About 150 people responded to the request, and 35 were invited to form a planning committee that met early the next month and created eight subcommittees to prepare action plans. The group was coordinated by an executive steering committee of one district person, three principals, and three teachers. Action plans explored six areas of concern:

- District mission statement

- Needs assessment

- Parent/community involvement

- Critical thinking skills

- Research on effective schools

- Resource support

The foundation agreed to review the group's work and conducted a site visit, and the executive committee continued planning through the summer of 1987. The foundation explained its hands-on strategy for technical assistance; a June meeting with the superintendent, the executive committee, and representatives from St. John's College was spent reviewing the improvement plan and deciding about next steps. The result was a commitment by the foundation to form a partnership and provide technical assistance and resources to support specific, mutually agreed-upon activities for school reform.

At that point, St. John's College arranged a series of meetings with Santa Fe's political, business, and community leaders, the State Education Department, and the superintendent. The foundation emphasized that efforts to promote site-based decision making in Santa Fe should be conducted in the context of the entire district, including schools, the school board, the superintendent, and the central office.

The Emergence of Lasting Reform Principles

In responding to the overture from St. John's College on behalf of the school system, the foundation communicated key points that have remained central to its partnerships:

- The foundation believed in (1) school-based reform and whole-school restructuring and (2) systemic, district-level reform.

- The foundation was interested in fundamental and long-term improvement, not short-term projects.

- The foundation did not have a preconceived model of schooling to impose, either directly or through subtle manipulation, although it did have beliefs and principles.

- The foundation was interested in helping schools develop and implement their own vision and plans for change.

- The foundation did not insist that every school or even any school participate in the partnership: participation by schools and individuals would be voluntary.

- The foundation trusted that teachers would play a central role in the district effort and in their own school reform programs.

- The foundation was prepared to commit human and financial resources over time to support a range of partnership activities that promised to foster restructuring. However, upon mutual agreement the partnership would be allowed to dissolve if either partner concluded that a relationship was no longer desirable.

Launching the Partnership

The foundation and the district launched the partnership in June 1987. Panasonic agreed to provide technical assistance to the district, drawing upon a pool of expert practitioners in addition to the foundation's senior consultants.

In August Santa Fe's mission statement on educational philosophy became the rationale for its School Improvement Program (SIP). Based on the Effective Schools Movement, which was the precursor to the current focus on restructuring, SIP engaged school staffs in setting goals and developing and implementing plans with the assistance of the foundation. With Panasonic's support, the superintendent had launched reform in Santa Fe.

The district, like the foundation, provided no particular models of schooling, no guidelines for schools to follow. The only requirement was that teachers initiate the changes after identifying school needs. Teachers were invited to develop and implement their own solutions to site problems, understanding that the partnership would support them in the process through technical assistance.

As Panasonic consultants faced this extraordinary opportunity, they soon found themselves sitting in schools with teams of teachers and sharing their knowledge of effective school improvement efforts. They helped teachers get ideas by sending them to professional conferences (on cooperative learning techniques, for example) and to exemplary schools and programs in other districts.

In some cases, the partnership sponsored on-site workshops featuring an array of school improvement ideas. They also held a two-day follow-up retreat for teachers to decide what options to pursue. When the basic skills teachers chose to develop interdisciplinary units, the partnership supported them. When Sweeney Elementary School teachers pursued multiage student groupings and governance through a teacher committee instead of a principal, the partnership helped. When Kearny Elementary School chose to combine first- and second-grade classes and use team teaching, the partnership assisted the staff in developing the idea and arranging for training.

Over several years, the foundation sponsored the following types of activities to foster school improvement:

- *visitations* to other school districts, such as middle school staff going to O'Farrell Community School in San Diego, or Santa Fe High School's site-based management team visiting schools in Irvine, California;

- *workshops* on such diverse topics as whole language, learning styles, site-based management, thematic instruction, promoting early literacy, special education inclusion, cooperative learning, interdisciplinary curriculum, conflict resolution, bilingual education, developmental learning, integrating art into the curriculum, and portfolio assessment;

- *retreats* for school faculties to study such topics as creating community in the school, block scheduling, staff evaluation, school self-assessment, multiage grouping, instructional teaming, and new program design;

- *professional conferences* on developing students' self-esteem, vocational education, the Comer model of school reform, and middle school philosophy; and

- *use of consultants* to work with schools on implementing specific strategies they had learned at workshops and conferences.

The foundation promoted a systematic process of self-study and improvement planning to empower teachers. For example, it introduced teachers to the *Middle Grades Assessment Program* to identify needs of middle school students and direction for program development. Panasonic funds supported such staff development activities as direct access to specific educational experts on request and interpretations and reviews of educational research on school reform. The story on Capital High School (see box, p. 56) illustrates this kind of school-level work.

A Crucial Lesson from the Start-up

The original executive committee monitored SIP team activities in the 25 schools during the 1987–88 school year. Evidence indicated much greater staff involvement in planning and decision making than ever before. For example, teachers and parents at two schools hired their own principals, with guidance from the central office.

The Gateways Program at Capital High School

Capital High School opened in 1988 to serve students who might have been less successful in the competitive atmosphere of the comprehensive Santa Fe High School and to relieve enrollment pressure from the growing population on the south side of town. Capital was planned as a shared-governance school, with the principal and a team of teachers on the governing council. The principal could, however, exercise his veto on policies developed by the school council, and frequently he did.

Meetings with Panasonic consultants opened teachers' minds to new ideas and opportunities, particularly during a four-day workshop that June prior to the school's opening. In exploring their concerns about traditional academic programs—especially honors courses that polarize students ethnically—teachers sought to organize the school without pull-out programs and with all students in academic courses. The result was a preliminary plan for an interdisciplinary humanities program, called Gateways.

However, for a number of reasons, the principal opened school that fall with all the familiar trappings of a conventional high school, including an honors program. Although Capital's Hispanic enrollment was 70 percent, 150 of 200 honors program students (75 percent) were Anglo.

Foundation staff met regularly with Capital teacher teams and kept in close touch by phone, urging them to respond to the challenge rather than accept the situation passively. In midyear, a core group of teachers decided to resurrect designs for the humanities program linking history, social studies, English, and language arts for all students. The Gateways block would occupy two and a half hours, with remaining time spent in mathematics, science, and the arts and electives. The program would offer "gateways" to understanding and controlling the historical, social, and artistic forces affecting students' lives.

Teachers piloted the fragile Gateways vessel through rough seas. Although the program needed four teachers, only two volunteered. The principal appointed two teachers who were generally acknowledged to be unsuited to an innovative humanities program, and neither wanted the assignment.

With encouragement and informal training from Panasonic consultants in asserting professional judgment, the staff developed teams for the following year and presented the principal with their plans. Gateways teachers also arranged to group classrooms physically to support program cohesion and foster interdisciplinary teaching.

The Hitachi Foundation funded a summer Gateways workshop. Panasonic sent members of the Gateways management team to visit successful restructuring schools and engaged curriculum and assessment experts to work with Gateways planners.

Gateways teachers gradually overcame many obstacles, such as administrators' and parents' suspicions about unfamiliar school structures, state requirements geared to traditional curriculum and instruction, and the existing culture of schooling. The strongest opposition was from parents of honors students, who worried that a heterogeneous program would hold their children back. Other teacher anxieties included fears of rejection by colleagues, reluctance to abandon texts, and concern that the superintendent would be unable to calm the community's and business leaders' fears. This concern about Superintendent Ortiz's public support was especially troubling, because he had always been supportive of such innovations. His support was critical because the superintendent decides which large-scale changes in curriculum and instruction require board approval. Unless he formally asked the school board to endorse Gateways, the program would be regarded as an unproven experiment—a deviation from the mainstream program.

(continued on page 58)

The foundation helped Gateways teachers acquaint the school board with the program and keep them informed. Teachers lobbied board members directly and invited them to see the program in operation; at least two of five board members visited.

When the superintendent still refused to put endorsement of Gateways on the board's agenda, foundation representatives discussed with him their concerns about undermining reform. This crucial meeting cleared the air, protecting the teachers' hard work and preserving the superintendent's leadership. The board officially endorsed Gateways at its spring 1991 meeting. As articles about the program appeared in the local news, the principal identified himself cautiously with its strengths.

Gateways' reputation spread as it won awards and recognition from the governors of New Mexico and Indiana. In 1991 all Gateways students except two special needs students passed the New Mexico Writing Competency Test, a feat never before achieved. Gateways was adopted as an exemplary program for Re:Learning states and received high praise from the renowned Coalition of Essential Schools.

Over the course of a few months, SIP addressed more topics than the system had in years: teacher empowerment, school-based management, scheduling, heterogeneous grouping, team teaching, interdisciplinary curriculum, alternative assessment, parent-community involvement, and climate. When teachers' ideas ran up against state education regulations, Ortiz appealed directly to legislators to amend standards in favor of improved educational practices. The chief obstacles to change appeared to be routine and manageable—mainly lack of time for planning and limited opportunities for training teachers and school administrators.

As the school system expanded and refined SIP, central office and school administrators raised a primary issue of distrust and complained that the superintendent had imposed SIP upon them. The reform process slowed while the foundation, the superintendent, and principals attempted to resolve this problem.

■

Stakeholders must become part of the solution
through a process of dialogue, and they must be included
in the dialogue from the outset.

The trust issue highlighted themes of subsequent Panasonic partnerships: stakeholders must become part of the solution through a process of dialogue, and they must be included in the dialogue from the outset. Santa Fe teachers and building administrators made it clear that they would not transform a school culture merely because visionary leaders state the need for school reform and indicate the path to achieving it. It is not enough to have "touched base" with stakeholders (a union, a key administrator, or board), nor is it possible to accomplish goals by going around these stakeholders or dealing with them later. The SIP experience also demonstrated that the task of enlisting all stakeholders in planning and establishing a partnership requires time, human and financial resources, and much dialogue before resistance erodes.

Reflections on Santa Fe

The foundation's decision to launch its Partnership Program in Santa Fe posed a special challenge because the school district was isolated culturally, economically, professionally, and geographically from the educational mainstream. Until the partnership began, the schools lacked substantive exposure to educational research, alternative models of schooling at any level, and financial resources to explore or implement innovative classroom practices.

A critical lesson was the importance of leadership from both the superintendent and the board of education. Superintendent Ortiz's unprecedented support of school improvement had propelled the SIP program, and his willingness to trust the various school management teams had created the need and the opportunity for the partnership. Yet his enthusiastic support did not preclude the need for working with other district leaders and developing their capacities to nurture reform.

The lack of involvement and commitment from the board of education was a real obstacle to reform. Although members had been informed about the partnership and its activities in the schools and across the district, interactions had been largely through Ortiz. The foundation had not developed a relationship with the board, so members did not strongly advocate the partnership.

■

Although board members change more frequently than superintendents, an ongoing relationship between the external assisters and the board helps to maintain the continuity of the partnership.

Based on this important lesson, Panasonic began to invest more of its resources and time with board members when developing new partnerships. The foundation meets with the board to help members better understand the principles on which it operates, the nature of a partnership, and the ways it will be working with the schools and the district. Although individual board members change more frequently than superintendents, an ongoing relationship helps to maintain the continuity of the partnership, even during a turbulent period of transition.

Santa Fe's leadership was to change twice over the partnership's life. The arrival in 1994–95 of a third superintendent—selected with the foundation's assistance and support—precipitated the end of the partnership. This superintendent was not only new to the district, but also new to the role of superintendent. She insisted on maintaining autonomous leadership, and she was willing to set aside the partnership, which she saw as interfering with her taking command of the district.

Panasonic ended the partnership reluctantly, despite strong support for the partnership among some groups in the district. The experience led the foundation to review accomplishments and clarify criteria for disengagement. Foundation staff and consultants had to face the fact that the superintendent is indeed the leader of a district, and that if they are not a partner with that leader, the partnership with the system cannot survive, just as a relationship with the board must reinforce the relationship with other district leaders. The foundation's investment in the Santa Fe "laboratory" generated perspective, skills, judgment, and, especially, a network of resources for effective technical assistance.

Chapter 4

Developing Capacity for Reform

*P*anasonic's educational philosophy is reflected in its mission, goals, and criteria for partnership commitment. The executive director and senior consultants begin each partnership by clarifying the foundation's perspective, its educational values, and what it does and does not stand for. Because of the disparities in practitioners' levels of knowledge across the districts, the foundation often assumes a mentorlike posture in the early stages of a partnership.

Panasonic's strategy for educational reform has been to cultivate partnerships whose success will depend on development of "capacity," that is, ability to create school conditions in which all children learn and teachers' efforts to foster learning are supported. The central idea behind a partnership is change in vision, roles, strategic directions, functions, infrastructure, assessment practices, accountability, use of data, and communications. These are delineated in the foundation's Framework for School System Success (see box and Appendix B for more detail).

As capacity builder, the foundation attempts to orient partner districts and schools toward a reform agenda that reflects the best research and successful practices in governance, management, teaching, and learning. Governance changes are a primary goal: Panasonic believes decisions should be made by those closest to students, so it places heavy emphasis on school-based decision making. The foundation also believes that district-level policies must be made with the involvement of school-based practitioners and the community;

hence, the emphasis on shared decision making and systemwide restructuring committees. Understanding that administrators and teachers are not likely to change practices and beliefs without information and training, the foundation supports extensive professional development and views it as a linchpin in its reform strategy.

Transferring knowledge is only a first step; transforming vision, professional and personal goals, and behaviors among practitioners is the more difficult task. This requires an ongoing negotiation process during which the partners come to know one another intimately. Over time, Panasonic's role in the partnership evolves from being a mentor to being a colleague. This process is not linear; it evolves by fits and starts and may regress due to a number of stressful factors, such as a change in the superintendency, as has occurred in half of the partnerships.

The Panasonic Foundation Framework for School System Success

1. A vision focused on equity and learning for all
2. Strategic direction based on learning and the centrality of the school as the place of learning
3. Clear delineation of roles, authority, and responsibilities
4. An infrastructure that enhances professional and organizational capacity
5. Assessment and evaluation practices aligned with learning standards and strategic direction
6. An accountability system focused on results
7. Effective use of well-managed data
8. Effective communications systems
9. Teachers unions and other professional associations as important system components
10. Meaningful engagement of system constituents and the broader community

(See Appendix B for full version.)

The partnership builds capacity for reform by conceiving, organizing, and carrying out a wide range of enabling activities. For example, at first a Panasonic consultant may "mastermind" a workshop, with the foundation identifying and enlisting experts to help district staff accomplish a particular goal, such as exploring authentic assessment or implementing school-based decision making. Over time, staff learn to identify and use resources with decreasing reliance on Panasonic. Sometimes the process goes fast, sometimes excruciatingly slow. It falters, or experiences a quantum jump. In an ideal partnership, the partners are expected ultimately to cut the apron strings entirely, as the district takes the lead.

Panasonic is still in the midst of this process in most partnership districts, and it is reluctant for this reason to estimate how long a partnership may take to achieve desired results. Five years? Ten years? It depends on a variety of factors and many unpredictable events.

Partnership capacity-building efforts in school-based decision making, staff development, and authentic assessment provide good examples of progress toward systemic reform. The partnerships' attempts to build capacity in these areas are described in this chapter. Although each of these areas is an important component of restructuring, the point of the process is not whether district staff acquire mastery in them, but whether staff are building the capacity to continue moving toward mastery on their own.

The three main sections of this chapter explain how Panasonic actively participates in and shapes the process of school reform. The process is difficult, time-consuming, labor-intensive, and sometimes frustrating and thankless. At the same time, the process can be gratifying when partnership growth and development—maturity—are evident. Ideally, a partner district will become a genuine colleague over time. This evolutionary process and its outcomes are illustrated as progress from dependency to collegial partnership in the following stories about school-based decision making in Lancaster, staff development in Allentown, and authentic assessment in Minneapolis.

School-Based Decision Making

In the belief that decision making at the school level should extend beyond school-based management, the foundation prefers the term *school-based decision making* (SBDM). In its Framework for School System Success (see box, p. 64, and Appendix B), the foundation asserts that schools should have autonomy to make budget allocation, personnel, schedule, curriculum, and instructional decisions designed to meet district performance standards.

■

We believe that decisions affecting the learning of children should be made, whenever possible, by those closest to children and be shared among those who must carry out the decisions. Only then can we expect teachers and school administrators to take responsibility for the education of their students.

—Panasonic Foundation

The foundation has provided extensive staff development and technical assistance to its partners as they go about implementing SBDM. Early partnership work in Minneapolis, for example, focused heavily on the district's restructuring efforts, which included SBDM. The Minneapolis School Board adopted site-based management guidelines in early 1992, and Panasonic assisted the district in training all school system staff in its definition, parameters, roles, and expectations, which are similar to those of SBDM. Collaborating with the local McKnight Foundation, the partnership assisted schools that responded to McKnight's 1991 and 1992 Requests for Proposals for Site-Based Reform Activities.

SBDM has been the pivotal issue for Panasonic's involvement with Lancaster, and it became the leverage point for mutual focus. Partnership activities there in 1994–95 exemplify the foundation's approach to developing systemwide capacity around restructuring. Although other major changes were occurring at the same time (e.g., a revised curriculum), the partnership was instrumental in moving district and school staff and board members toward SBDM. Over time, staff started to understand the processes and structure of SBDM, and many schools established councils to implement it.

At the outset Lancaster was struggling to implement school-based management: the superintendent hoped Panasonic would help "get his vision picked up by building managers." During the initial Panasonic-Lancaster conversation in April 1994, key district staff spoke the "language of reform," but different people defined its terms differently. Also, in references to SBDM, schoolpeople did not naturally include the community and parents, but focused on sharing between the district and the schools. Finally, schoolpeople needed to learn how to implement SBDM.

Some management decisions had already been delegated to principals, and some schools had committees of teachers deciding specific issues. The high school, for example, had a faculty council acting as a leadership group. The school also had $150,000 in discretionary funds to control. The teachers union reported, however, that principals were still making singular decisions about the allocation of these discretionary funds rather than diffusing authority—and responsibility—throughout the schools.

Principals were concerned about the overall lack of knowledge about SBDM: they thought staff needed exposure to school systems that had already implemented it. The school board, which thought its role was to set parameters for SBDM, had mandated a pilot in several schools in 1994–95 and full implementation in 1995–96.

Panasonic recommended that a broad-based group representing school constituencies lead the reform and urged the superintendent to restate his commitment to participatory management at the district's annual Leadership Team Training that June. He asked his principals to start working toward SBDM, but their reactions indicated general confusion.

At a foundation-facilitated superintendent's cabinet retreat in August 1994, a Panasonic consultant asked each member to state his or her particular goal for SBDM.

- The district's partnership liaison, an elementary school principal, wanted to set parameters on SBDM and learn more about its process.

- The administrative director wanted to define Panasonic's role in Lancaster that year and for the future and learn how Panasonic fit into the district's plans. He wanted to know the leadership skills needed at every level to implement SBDM and asked about Panasonic's agenda.

- The curriculum director wanted parameters and timelines for SBDM and a plan for evaluating it. She felt the term needed to be clearly defined and commonly understood, and that legal and contractual constraints that would define and limit the extent to which it could be implemented had to be identified and factored in before the schools became involved.

- The superintendent's senior assistant wanted to know what SBDM is and which other districts use it.

- The superintendent wanted to tie everything together.

These are typical issues and concerns for educators engaged in change. The group eventually agreed that key tasks were to manage the reform and plan a participatory activity. Panasonic gave out copies of Minneapolis's school-based management document and suggested the cabinet use it as a framework. The cabinet next formed an interim steering committee to define the parameters of school reform and plan the partnership's unleashing event.

The interim committee met several times in September and October of 1994 to plan for an "Enlarged Committee" with representatives from every school. At its first meeting in November, the group agreed on five key goals, one of which was to develop SBDM parameters for the district. The group also selected school representatives to work with the interim steering committee on Super Tuesday, the partnership's unleashing event in Lancaster.

The relation of shared decision making to curriculum was the primary concern of teachers who participated in Super Tuesday. A third of the sessions examined related topics, and several issues and questions were raised repeatedly:

- How does SBDM relate to changes in instruction?

- SBDM doesn't mean the principal gives up all authority, but must she or he become an instructional leader?

- Since many staff will be assigned to different schools as the new high school building opens and junior highs become middle schools, is it premature to be implementing SBDM with current assignments?

- What is the role of district curriculum staff?

- What kinds of decisions will central administrators be willing to relinquish to sites? How will they manage and support the process?

- What district and state constraints exist, and where are waivers needed?

A "parameters subcommittee" of the Enlarged Committee began meeting in January 1995 to establish parameters for school councils to follow in implementing SBDM. Members raised concerns about governance and decision making, ownership, inclusion/participation, school support mechanisms, communications, and coordination. When several participants said they did not know what parameters were, the Panasonic consultant facilitating the meeting distributed samples of parameters and focused the group on developing definitions.

Meanwhile, at a retreat facilitated by Panasonic, the school board planned to do the following:

- shift budget decisions to the schools;

- allocate time and resources so staff could plan, implement, and evaluate their collaborative work; and

- provide for policy waivers and exceptions.

That March, Panasonic sponsored a team-building workshop for 130 staff from the district's schools to help them see connections between effective decision making, effective team interaction, and school and district restructuring. After hearing the reactions and questions of participants (e.g., What happens when a site does not approve a systemwide decision?), the consultant running the workshop reported:

> It is important to create more local capacity within the district for site teams to get continuous and frequent support and consultation as they try out new processes for decision making. The traditional places schools look for support—central office or professional development offices—may or may not be prepared currently to provide that support, as it seems they have had no more interaction with the ideas than others in the district.

A second training event for the Enlarged Committee on site council development was led by a school-based budgeting expert from the Dade County Public Schools in Florida. Another Panasonic consultant who attended made the following observation:

> I'm struck by the sense that both district-level and school-level people seem to view site-based reform as a "zero-sum" game rather than a "value-added" proposition. The question they're primarily focusing on seems to be "Which things that the district does now might be taken back or taken over by the schools?" rather than "What good things might happen that aren't happening now if schools are empowered with new capacities?" The zero-sum view is somewhat impoverished not only because it focuses pretty much on "instrumental" activities (doing purchase orders, etc.) but because it rather completely embraces/endorses the status quo as the "field of play." The value-added view assumes that a range of beneficial possibilities that aren't currently being imagined or realized at any level of the system, whether school or district, might be "invented" by schools if they're supported by the system in the right sorts of ways.

Partnership consultants needed to find ways to enhance the understandings of school representatives, district staff, and the board. They felt by the end of the school year that the superintendent's cabinet had taken conceptual charge of the reform process but still needed to accept management responsibility. One observer stated:

> *There seemed to be a marked contrast between the way central office personnel talked about SBDM in June and on Super Tuesday last November. Then central office directors, coordinators, and specialists were guarded—pointing out many obstacles and potential problems that would arise if site-based committees had too much freedom to decide instructional issues. Now these persons seem genuinely comfortable with the site-based arrangements that are emerging. These arrangements are set up to preserve the state and district levels of goal setting and procedures as appropriate, while encouraging a high level of school-by-school involvement in implementation. It is clear that working out the parameters for SBDM has forced many central office personnel, principals, and teachers to think hard about how what they want and believe about schooling relates to people in other positions and levels.*

Panasonic worked with the district's curriculum director to plan for comprehensive school assistance in light of SBDM parameters. It worked with the parameters subcommittee to establish a working set of parameters for board approval and distribution to schools. It planned with the Enlarged Committee to set up a replacement districtwide council for the fall.

Lancaster decided to devote its two August staff development days to SBDM training for all of its schools. The partnership liaison requested that Panasonic facilitators assist the schools in developing "indicators of success" for common vision and goals, climate, community, student success, and shared leadership and responsibility to achieve student success. The Enlarged Committee would then construct a "districtwide framework for evaluating and supporting site-based management." The superintendent's assistant told the Enlarged Committee: "I think August 28th is the most crucial day in our site-based initiative. This day must be successful. Every site has to understand why they are engaging in the activity, and every site needs to produce a product."

The foundation eventually agreed to provide ten consultants (four from the Allentown Partnership) and train ten Lancaster staff to

Parameters for Decentralized Decision Making

1. All sites must have a procedure for keeping everyone informed and involved. This includes a description of communication strategies, e.g., newsletters, meetings, debriefings, appropriate for all faculty, staff, and school community.

2. Site-based decisions will be inherently defined as an inclusive and shared process of decision making.

3. All stakeholders must be represented on all committees engaged in the decision-making process.

4. Decisions by any school which significantly affect another school must be negotiated or gain informed consent.

5. Any systemwide decision that affects the decisions and operations of school sites must be made through a process of negotiation and consent by the sites.

6. A process will be put in place and defined by the "enlarged group" to assist school sites with the following:
   - seeking ways to accomplish decisions within the laws, policies, and contracts affecting the district
        (if not)
   - seeking waiver(s) from such laws, policies, or contracts
        (if not)
   - helping the site to implement its decisions in an alternative way.

—Lancaster, February 1995

work with individual school teams at the August in-service session. This would ensure that local teachers developed ownership of the indicators and standards for which they would be responsible. Before the new school year began, the foundation met with the superintendent's cabinet to discuss the next phase: a districtwide council; follow-up on the schools' indicators work; and Panasonic's work with individual schools on school-based budgeting, site council development, and collaborative decision making.

These accomplishments were substantial for a partnership in its infancy. Despite the long road ahead, Lancaster had made great strides toward achieving a goal requiring widespread commitment and capacity building.

Staff Development

Super Tuesdays and Saturdays, summer institutes, workshops, school retreats, and cross-site visitations: these constitute forums for the staff development that Panasonic believes is so vital to school reform. Practitioners must have ideas, training to translate ideas into action, and the desire to broaden their vision and understanding.

■

*Understanding that administrators and teachers are
not likely to change practices and beliefs without information and training,
the partnerships support extensive professional development
as a linchpin in the reform strategy.*

The Allentown Partnership, for example, has developed the ability to plan and sponsor an annual, week-long Summer Restructuring Workshop for the district's practitioners and parents. Foundation consultants played a major role in planning the first few workshops, but by the fourth, the district's School Council Coordinating

Committee (SCCC) was able to plan almost independently. The SCCC has told much of its own story.

> *In December 1990 the Panasonic Foundation and the Allentown School District began working with a volunteer cadre of teachers, parents, and school principals to plan a districtwide restructuring conference for the spring, 1991. Teachers at each level—elementary, middle, and high school—spent a day attending workshops on restructuring ideas and themes. Panasonic provided practitioners and consultants from around the country who aimed at expanding staff vision. The success of the conference led to increased requests for technical assistance for restructuring efforts and a desire on the volunteers' part to continue to work together as a group.*

> *At a November 1991 SCCC meeting, intensive summer workshops were recommended to improve education at the school site. The group then helped plan a four-day summer restructuring workshop in 1992 that offered staff a variety of themes, ideas, and advice on reforming and restructuring schools.*

> *In October 1992, the newly appointed superintendent met with the voluntary cadre for a full-day retreat ... subcommittees were formed in policy/bylaws, communications, curriculum, and staff development. A summer restructuring workshop was planned that required a school-based planning focus. School teams, composed of teachers, parents, principals, and a community and business representative, submitted proposals to the SCCC describing what their school wanted to accomplish at the four-day summer workshop in June 1993. Each school also met for a day in August to follow up on the June workshop and to prepare plans to implement ideas fostered in that workshop.*

—SCCC, 12/93

During that time period, Panasonic and the local Rider-Pool Foundation were still heavily involved in planning. In February 1992, for example, Panasonic consultants held afternoon meetings with representatives from every school in the district to plan the four-day June workshop. A Summer Workshop Committee (the staff development subcommittee of the SCCC) met again with foundation consultants in March and April as planning progressed. Panasonic's involvement in planning the summer 1993 workshop was just as intense; in addition to maintaining frequent contact by phone, a senior consultant traveled to Allentown once a month from January to June to assist the SCCC in developing and distributing a request for proposals for workshop topics to the schools, reviewing proposals, planning sessions, and identifying consultants from the foundation's network to run the workshops. This process was first conducted in Santa Fe as a mechanism to encourage the transfer of knowledge.

Panasonic's staff development assistance had become the linchpin for professional development in the district. However, the foundation wanted the district to take over the process, asking for Panasonic's feedback only on workshop topics and experts to teach them. An observer's notes from the May 1993 staff development subcommittee meeting depicts the following scene:

> A number of the regular SCCC representatives—about 10— stayed for the subcommittee meeting, which focused on the June 1993 summer training. One rep suggested that presenters write out their goals, objectives, and syllabi for staff to see prior to training. This would insure people are getting what they want. The Panasonic consultant suggested presenters do this on the blackboard the first day of training. The rep disagreed, and his suggestion was accepted by the group.

School staff who participate in the summer training are required to develop a plan to implement the training in their schools. The Panasonic consultant suggested participants "make full use" of the consultants who do the training by scheduling time to meet and work with them in the afternoon and evening.

The subcommittee endorsed a 1994 summer workshop at its November 1993 meeting, noting that Panasonic had expressed interest in participating in it.

The Staff Development subcommittee discussed some improvements for the 1994 workshop:

- *Have a training course for the school contact person.*

- *Send out course descriptions to each school.*

- *Assess each school's needs and prepare a list of suggested topics that will be available at the workshop.*

Topics still under discussion for January:

- *Themes to be presented.*

- *Location (is Trexler Middle School available for us?).*

- *Review our sign-up and evaluation forms.*

- *What to do about schools that do not have parental involvement.*

- *Will presenters be local or from Panasonic?*

A foundation consultant met with the subcommittee in February and April of 1994 to discuss the format of the summer workshop and to help the group review school proposals and organize sessions.

That fall the subcommittee started working with the SCCC's curriculum subcommittee and enlisted a nationally known educator to

Exciting New Programs and Practices to Change the Way Students Learn

The halls of Trexler Middle School were alive with enthusiasm and determination as schools initiated programs which will change the face of education in Allentown for years to come. At a workshop held in June, teams from each of Allentown's 23 schools worked on exciting new programs that were being considered for inclusion in the 1994–95 school year.

The School Council Coordinating Committee, in cooperation with the Allentown School District, Panasonic Foundation, Rider-Pool Foundation, and the Allentown Education Association, sponsored the Third Annual Summer Restructuring Workshop. The purpose of the workshop was to assist schools in restructuring processes which focus on child-centered changes. The participants, almost 450 of them, included administrators, teachers, parents, paraprofessionals, and community members.

In early spring, Requests for Proposals from school teams outlined restructuring plans and included requests for summer workshop topics. With the assistance of the Panasonic Foundation, appropriate consultants were scheduled and school contact persons selected. Highlighting opening-day activities was keynote speaker Paul Schwarz of Central Park East Secondary School in New York, a school well known for its innovative, child-centered approach.

—*SCCC Special Edition*, Allentown School District, Fall 1994 run a session on interdisciplinary curriculum in response to teachers' interest. This was a first step for the district in relying on its own network to staff the next summer workshop.

The Panasonic consultant wrote at a February 1995 subcommittee meeting that planners

> *needed little help from us to move the process along ... [because] the workshop was being built around the model already established. This promoted efficiency, as the group could focus on weaknesses in the previous effort, knowing that basically the design was feasible and productive.*

By the summer of 1995, Allentown had held four annual Summer Restructuring Workshops, planned and conducted by members of the SCCC and its staff development subcommittee. Panasonic was intimately involved in this planning from the beginning but over time watched the SCCC take on increasingly more responsibility.

Attended by teams from each school, the 1995 workshop featured four days of interactions with consultants provided by the foundation from its nationwide network. A fifth day was spent planning for implementation in individual schools.

In preparation for the workshop, teams from each school submitted proposals indicating the topic they wanted to explore for implementation as part of their overall school improvement plan. The foundation worked with the SCCC to secure expert consultants and to organize a schedule that allowed schools to (1) learn about new programs, instructional methods, or school organizational strategies and (2) work as a team to prepare for sharing with the rest of the faculty and for implementation. Topics included team building and managing shared governance (for schools near the beginning of the process), multiage grouping, inclusion of special needs students in regular instruction, manipulatives-based math instruction, alternative methods of student assessment, and integrated curriculum.

Teachers responded to the high quality of consultants' presentations: they were very involved in discussions, development of guidelines for schools, preparation of curriculum and materials, and planning for how to deal with student behavior and mobility. It was the kind of staff training week every district should have.

A high school principal commented that the restructuring workshops have "opened the eyes of many teachers. People are coming forward. They are beginning to believe in themselves. When Panasonic brings advisors from other school districts, our teachers see they too can become change agents." The foundation believes the district can continue to evolve on its own, especially with the $300,000 per year the school board now allocates for staff development.

Authentic Assessment

For Panasonic, authentic assessment of student progress is fundamental to school restructuring because it generally measures what students learn more accurately and fully than standardized tests. It means measuring students' academic performance directly through multiple demonstrations of learning, rather than indirectly through pencil-and-paper, multiple-choice tests. While use of authentic assessments encourages the teaching of thinking and problem-solving skills, use of standardized tests in school districts for accountability purposes tends to induce "teaching to the test."

By assessing students' performance on complex and meaningful tasks, authentic assessment is a way of focusing attention on challenging standards. Authentic assessments also force educators into a new level of consciousness about curriculum and instruction:

they need to know what classroom experiences children must have to develop appropriate skills.

When a group of teachers in Santa Fe was invited to design a new elementary school that would open as Turquoise Trail in 1990, Panasonic worked with the teachers to develop the new school's philosophy of "active learning, thematic curriculum, heterogeneous grouping, and *appropriate assessment*." Foundation consultants helped Turquoise Trail's teachers develop measures such as a portfolio system, a narrative report card, and performance assessments in mathematics.

In the late 1980s, Panasonic helped San Diego's O'Farrell Community School develop into an exemplary middle school by providing technical assistance that included authentic assessment. O'Farrell's ultimate goal for graduates is measured through an eighth-grade portfolio presentation and a multidimensional project that demonstrates student progress.

The foundation's assessment work in Minneapolis dates back to 1989–90, when the foundation sponsored a partnershipwide conference on authentic assessment and a workshop in Minneapolis that sparked the establishment of a Student Assessment Committee. Authentic assessment continued to be an issue, culminating in an intense series of planning activities in 1994–95.

In June 1995 the school board approved the "Strategic Direction for Assessment," based on groundwork laid at a two-day planning conference in April (see box, p. 84). The process leading up to board approval of a new direction for assessment illustrates Panasonic's approach: focusing attention at critical moments; encouraging discussion; providing experts and resources; and ensuring district follow-through. The foundation provided national assessment experts to lead the April conference and a summer seminar for principals and school teams ("How Do We Measure Up?"), and cosponsored a summer assessment workshop for middle school teachers.

Public Strategies Group (PSG), the private firm hired to provide leadership services to the Minneapolis Public Schools, had a results-based contract. Its annual payments depended on PSG meeting a series of measurable student goals, with an emphasis on standardized test scores, but also with an expectation that "a greater variety of student measures" would be developed.

District and school staff became engaged in what many dubbed "the holy war," that is, strong philosophical disagreement about how student achievement should be measured. Those who favored the continued use of standardized tests argued that in order to validly report student achievement, they needed tried-and-true measures as the PSG contract required. Others saw the potential in new, authentic measures of student achievement, such as portfolios and performance assessments. Several had already developed and piloted alternative assessments in Minneapolis, and they now saw them as sitting on the back burner.

Panasonic had been urging a districtwide change to authentic assessment for more than three years. In a 1991 letter to the superintendent, the executive director indicated Panasonic would "provide technical assistance to the district for the development of performance assessment measures." Finally in 1994, Panasonic was able to support an expert study of Minneapolis's assessment system. Two nationally known measurement experts reviewed the authentic assessments that had been developed in the district and also analyzed the existing standardized testing program. Chief among their recommendations were that (1) more research was needed on the alternative assessments that had been developed and (2) the district should do less standardized testing in certain grades (LeMahieu and Mehrens, 1994).

Since a plan for dealing with the report's recommendations had not been developed, the foundation embarked on several months of discussions with the superintendent and district assessment staff. People on all sides of the issue took the opportunity for open discussion; some hoped that concrete strategies would be identified, while others feared the possible changes that would result. Foundation consultants told the superintendent they wanted the April conference to end with definite plans; he assured them their work was "right on track" and that decisions would be made.

■

People on all sides of the assessment issue took the opportunity for open discussion; some hoped that concrete strategies would be identified, while others feared the possible changes that would result.

The purpose of the April conference was to "develop a draft strategic direction for student assessment and a plan for communicating the assessment strategy." Panasonic hoped a philosophy, strategy, and direction for assessment would be determined. Expert presenters set a context for discussion of authentic assessment issues and led participants in a series of activities to clarify their positions and recommendations. The conference ended with a list of attributes that a new strategic direction for assessment should include and ideas for communicating these to others. Panasonic urged staff follow-up so that recommendations would be implemented.

That summer, the partnership ran a seminar for principals and teams of teachers to provide an understanding of the national context and examples of authentic assessments already being used in Minneapolis schools and elsewhere. An August workshop for middle school teams also focused on assessment.

A new climate around authentic assessment exists in Minneapolis, in part due to Panasonic's work. The expert study, the April confer-

Strategic Direction for Assessment

An assessment system with the following attributes will best meet the needs of the Minneapolis Public Schools stakeholders:

■ Assessments should be linked explicitly to the Minneapolis curriculum content standards.

■ The system should include a combination of assessment methods, measures, and analysis developed internally and independently (e.g., from national or regional sources).

■ There should be multiple assessment tools (e.g., portfolio, demonstration, and observation) available for measuring student performance on various learning outcomes, including: factual knowledge and process skills; problem solving and thinking skills; application and integration skills; and communication and task management skills.

■ A mix of assessment instruments should be used: some districtwide, some schoolwide, most for individual students or classrooms. Regardless, all tools should be explicitly linked to the curriculum content standards.

Pursuing the assessment strategy outlined above will require:

■ Trust among all stakeholders for new methods and approaches to assessment as they complement or perhaps replace older, established methods.

■ Professional development for those who design assessments as well as those who will use them to support improved student achievement.

■ Curriculum content standards and related assessments that together are more reliable, challenging, relevant, and useful in summarizing what students learn and are able to do than the combination of measures currently available.

■ A well-planned transition period so that a void of assessment information never exists.

—Excerpted from the Minneapolis Public Schools'
"Strategic Direction for Assessment," June 13, 1995

ence, the board policy, the principals' leadership retreat, and the middle school teachers' assessment workshop—all supported by the partnership—are signs that the district is seriously moving toward authentic assessment and building staff capacity to continue development and implementation of it.

The Meaning of Capacity Building

These stories about building local capacity to plan and sponsor SBDM, professional development, and new approaches to assessment indicate that several levels of organization and structure must be tapped to ensure progress. The districts played integral roles in all three instances, carrying out board mandates (in Lancaster), establishing frameworks for systemwide discussion of an important topic (in Minneapolis and Lancaster), or creating a formal structure for districtwide, representative decision making (in Allentown). Individual schools played important roles in Allentown and Lancaster, where school representatives were formal decision makers, or where schools were required to implement a new decision-making structure.

The foundation has introduced formal change mechanisms, resources, experts, and research-based information into the mix of events and activities in each district. Its purpose has been to initiate, inform, enable, and provide funds for schoolpeople to begin a process and then take it over. The provision of such opportunities is vitally important to systemic reform, just as developing local capacity is a requirement for sustaining reform.

Chapter 5

Allentown, Pennsylvania— Leading and Managing Change

T he process of selecting a superintendent of schools sends powerful messages throughout a community, focusing attention on educational issues and challenges that affect not only students, parents, and school staff, but the business community and political leadership as well. Even more than a school board election, selecting a leader for the schools clarifies and tests the values of the school board, forces it to publicly declare priorities, and indicates the direction in which the school system is headed.

The superintendent selection process offers opportunities for the school community to rethink fundamental assumptions, redefine its mission, and clarify expectations. It communicates the school board's perception of change and its concept of the qualities of leadership required to define and meet new challenges. Finally, it tests the board's willingness to invest time, effort, and resources to seek and hire the most capable leader available.

As the process begins, the school board confronts basic questions: Is the mission of new leadership to preserve continuity? To restore traditional stability? Or to define and meet needs for improvement?

School districts and their communities often fail to seize these opportunities. School boards may not perceive them and may focus instead on specific, symptomatic problems. Decision makers may set their sights too low, failing to notice possibilities and concentrating on short-term objectives. Systems may lack the capacity to explore educational issues involved in selecting a leader. And systems may lack a means to create and manage a thoroughgoing selection process.

■

A community must envision what its school district should look like over time and what kind of superintendent will move the district toward its vision.

Allentown, Pennsylvania, offered a classic case of the small city suddenly facing big-city dilemmas concentrated and most visible in its public schools. Allentown's search for a new superintendent in 1992 provided an opportunity for Panasonic to (1) help shape a process to define the characteristics of the superintendent and (2) urge inclusion of critical stakeholders within and beyond the district in the decision. The foundation's goal was to clarify and reaffirm the district's direction and help identify a person to continue its reform efforts.

A Small City Confronts Big-City Problems

Like several small cities in eastern Pennsylvania, Allentown has historically fit the image of a tranquil working-class community—a city of about 100,000, including 13,500 public school students. The school district has long taken pride in its 23 orderly schools, predictable rates of college entrance, success with traditional students, reputation for outstanding marching bands, teachers who had themselves been students in the local schools, and good relations with the community.

Historically, the private sector had driven the economy and determined the social structure, including governmental and social services of the region. Two corporations—Mack Trucks and Air Products and Chemicals—acted as philanthropists, social agencies, and employers in Allentown until the early 1980s, when Mack Trucks left, seeking cheaper labor. The region experienced the full impact of the economic recession with plant closings, taxpayer revolts, and budget cuts. Over a decade, Allentown replaced 12,000 high-wage industrial jobs with 16,000 lower-wage service jobs.

An influx of single-parent, low-income families from New York City in the early 1990s exacerbated problems associated with large inner cities—an increase in the teen pregnancy rate (10 percent of Allentown babies are born to teenage mothers), AIDS, drugs, disruptive and unstable youth, and many difficulties posed by language and cultural barriers. Stark contrasts in social norms soured community relations. Even more distressing, these problems—which many believe Allentown is unprepared to handle—are expected to increase rapidly as this population doubles within the decade.

Allentown school officials cited many challenges: some schools experienced almost 50 percent annual turnover of students, dropout rates were rising, and students did not seem to be learning. The district was having great difficulty adapting to changing conditions, and the schools' decline began to undermine long-held confidence in traditional school practices. As one administrator explained, "Many of our teachers were hired in the old days before Allentown became a real urban district. We don't have the experience, training, and support to deal with the new challenges."

The school board president saw concrete reasons for community concern and recalled that in eight years as a board member, he had not been involved in a single expulsion hearing, yet in the past year he had attended nine, all related to weapons in school. One teacher expressed a growing sense of desperation: "We are hanging on now, but we don't know how much longer we can go on like this."

Partly in response to such problems, the teachers union led school reform by including in their contract the "Allentown Accord," which required school-based management (SBM) by councils composed of teachers, administrators, parents, and community members. As one administrator defined SBM, "The central administration and board are supposed to set the priorities, and we are supposed to decide how to implement them." The union worked hard to focus schools on instructional improvement, and the district provided extensive training for school site councils.

Panasonic Explores a Partnership with Allentown

The superintendent at that time, Richard Cahn, an advocate of school reform, approached Panasonic with a request for help with the Allentown Accord, and for training in school-based management, instructional leadership, the role of parents on school councils, and assessment strategies.

The foundation's senior staff declined to help with the Accord specifically, largely because the foundation is concerned with system-level restructuring. While the superintendent's request to the foundation focused on training for teachers, parents, and principals, Panasonic's response targeted training for central office staff to assume changing roles in ensuring the long-term success of school-based reform. Panasonic had learned from other partnerships that central office staff must be trained to serve "not simply as facilitators, but also as advocates and provocateurs" of the initiative. Between 1989 and 1991 the foundation team visited Allentown periodically, seeking an opportunity to join forces in restructuring.

Attempts to help the district convert curriculum specialists into generalists on whole-school reform led nowhere. In March 1991 a senior Panasonic consultant concluded:

The superintendent is far ahead of the rest of the district. The more time I spend with him, the greater my appreciation for the difficult conditions under which he works. For him, reform is an uphill battle.... While several members of the Board of School Directors give support to what they call "school-based reform," some of them actually mean they would like schools to go through the motions of deciding about cosmetic issues, and nothing else. On the district level, the superintendent and union president are lonely advocates of fundamental reform.

The superintendent did have an opportunity to encourage school reform at an early partnership workshop. He promised to provide whatever was needed to a middle school that wanted to reform. Panasonic acted as go-between, trusted by both sides, neither of which trusted the other. Panasonic's role was to convey each side's position accurately to the other. The consultant would ask the superintendent, "Did you say the middle school has your permission to revise its schedule and modify its budget categories?" And the consultant would tell the school, "You heard it—you have that permission, now the ball is in your court."

The school planned to change its schedule and teach in teams. The plan exceeded the budget and otherwise broke rules, but the superintendent kept his promise.

The partnership then accelerated in an attempt to capitalize on this visible example of collaboration. The superintendent later reflected on these early events in a letter to Panasonic's executive director.

Initially, Panasonic gave us the confidence to do what we believed was necessary to improve schools by confirming and clarifying with us what it was we believed. Our convictions were structured and given direction. Part of this time was spent in repeated and necessary discussions with district leaders, includ-

ing our union president and me; part of this phase was the very, very encouraging opportunity to meet with others—district people and experts from across the country—who were doing what was only a vision for me. That too was excellent, timely.

An early and great difficulty in what we were doing in our change process was addressed by Panasonic: the emphasis here was all on process and, while our people were talking to each other about students and learning, nothing was happening. Panasonic provided information, consultants, linkages with other districts, and in-service and consultation which presented ideas and programs that were already working somewhere to improve student learning, i.e., change "ideas" which suggested needs to our people. Many of the initiatives with substance in the district can be connected to Panasonic.

It is fortunate for Allentown that Panasonic has been willing to get involved where "the rubber hits the road," as it were. Allentown was not equipped with the change capability to have the appropriate people involved in the important decisions. The immediate issue here was neither knowledge retrieval nor funding. It was one of values, on what matters with youngsters; on respect for ourselves to get involved; and on a conviction that youngsters could do better, that we were not getting the job done.... Panasonic has been an internal change agent, functioning and accepted as part of the district. Neat!

After months of negotiation to build on the middle school success story, Panasonic launched the Allentown Partnership with a signature unleashing event—a Super Saturday for the entire district staff, a full day of professional development on restructuring. Panasonic pulled together the School Council Coordinating Committee (SCCC) to plan the workshop. The SCCC consists of representatives from all 23 school site councils and plays an indispensable role, enabling schools to communicate with each other. It holds monthly meetings of the whole, maintains several subcommittees, and publishes a newsletter.

The SCCC provides a vehicle outside of traditional district and school structures for planning, communication, and coordination. Through the SCCC, the schools have a voice in the district and in traditional district functions. Because the SCCC fulfills a need expressed wherever schools are beginning to change and want mutual support, foundation consultants frequently refer to it as a model.

Two Foundations Seize an Opportunity

The foundation discovered a local ally, the Rider-Pool Foundation, which had funded efforts to promote SBM, but, working alone, had been unable to have a significant impact on substantive educational reform in Allentown. While Panasonic and Rider-Pool mulled over ways to help address Allentown's problems in late 1991, the superintendent suddenly resigned after the election of three non-sympathetic board members.

■

*While Panasonic and Rider-Pool mulled over ways
to help address Allentown's problems in late 1991,
the superintendent suddenly resigned.*

The two foundations watched in dismay as the Allentown school board struggled with the superintendent selection process. The board would not spend money on a search. One member expressed the predominant mood: "We don't have to go for the best superintendent we can find. It will cost too much, and besides, we don't need the best."

Panasonic and Rider-Pool decided this was an opportunity for change if they could open up the search process to involve more stakeholders in a public conversation to explore and act upon important issues. Together they would make it possible for the community to envision what the district should look like over time and what kind of superintendent would move the district toward its vision. Panasonic would sponsor research and public discussion, and Rider-Pool would provide $5,000 to fund a nationwide search. In February 1992, the school board accepted both offers.

Foundation consultants assisted in a community and staff survey and sponsored a school board retreat to formally determine the selection process, which was to insure a voice for teachers, administrators, and community members. This process helped board members seek the kind of superintendent indicated by the survey—a new leader committed to the reform process and continuing school improvement.

The two foundations showed exceptional timing, strategy, and diplomacy, and appropriate assertiveness. They helped identify a focused superintendent who had relevant experiences and background to advance reforms. With broad support from all stakeholder groups because they had participated in the selection process, she would also have support for the reform agenda.

Accelerating Change with a New Superintendent

The new superintendent, who started in October 1992, worked on several fronts, frequently with Panasonic's assistance and always inviting close communication. After personally conducting focus groups on academic standards, the superintendent developed a community vision for the schools, involving the entire community in writing a consensus statement. She also invited a representative mix of community members to a series of Saturday conferences. A futurist speaker would stimulate the audience to consider possibilities on a topic, and participants would explore the topic in small groups to reach consensus. Hired in part on the strength of her commitment to school-based management, the superintendent led four town meetings on that topic and produced a "white paper" to encourage continuing discussion and action on school reform.

The foundation has deepened its association with the Allentown schools since then. The pace of change has quickened. Individual school communities are rethinking how to operate schools so that every child can learn at a high level; more than half of the elementary schools are seriously attempting new approaches, such as including special education students in regular classrooms and redesigning reading instruction; initiatives in the four middle schools include team teaching and new forms of assessment; and high schools are experimenting with small "families" of students and teachers who work in teams.

In one major collaborative activity, a foundation consultant experienced in school-business partnerships enabled the business community and the school board to collaborate in developing a shared vision for the school district through the Allentown Leadership Alliance. The consultant helped the Alliance—a planning group of corporate leaders and university presidents—to understand they were contributing to the establishment of goals, not simply endorsing goals the district had already determined.

The Alliance has a dual purpose: to broaden community involvement with and support for the schools, and to develop the community's capacity to support reform efforts without relying on Panasonic Foundation resources. The Alliance hopes eventually to develop the capacity and the motivation to coordinate the role of business in the district.

Allocating Foundation Resources

One issue the foundation faces in every partnership is that of strategically allocating resources. It has provided approximately $100,000 per year to foster restructuring in Allentown—a substantial sum for the foundation, but a fraction of the district's budget.

As the foundation and the district considered how to use limited funds most effectively, Panasonic staff viewed requests for assistance and funds as opportunities to examine the rationale behind each request. The overriding questions became: Is there a way to use funds to increase the pressure for change, and is honoring this request going to create that pressure? To accelerate change, district and foundation staff established priorities, first supporting schools that sought to deepen and extend their progress or schools that were focusing on a single goal that contributed to the overall reform effort. As requests increased, the superintendent and Panasonic developed a schedule of assistance using a team coordinated by a senior foundation consultant. The foundation also began seeking consultants with enough expertise and a broad vision to promote rapid restructuring.

Breaking Molds

One of the most difficult challenges facing a partnership is how to change entrenched ways of thinking. Concerned that resistance based on traditional thinking could prevent restructuring of individual schools, foundation staff encouraged the superintendent to develop ways of working with failing schools that do not change.

The superintendent found one lever in principals' performance reviews, achieving consensus in a meeting of principals to set clear leadership goals by which they might be judged. The group agreed that one goal must be to lead the school council through proper development and the school through the changes involved in reform.

The selection of principals by school site councils has been an opportunity for the district to promote change and build trust among parents and community representatives. Committees of 15 to 20 diverse people come to know the superintendent personally and are challenged to seek candidates whose leadership capabilities will meet expectations created by a new, shared vision of educational possibilities.

■

The selection of principals by school site councils has been
an opportunity for the district to promote change and build trust
among parents and community representatives.

Collaboration between Panasonic consultants and the district resulted in a union-district waiver from the contract and from district personnel rules. Under their contract, teachers cannot be paid while on leave; their salary is used to hire a long-term substitute. When one of Allentown's schools lost a key reading teacher to maternity leave, a waiver was negotiated to allow the school to hire the teacher as a part-time consultant, and a teaching aide for the rest of the time.

The superintendent and teachers union also exploited opportunities for reform when they agreed to convert a traditional system of reimbursement for university courses into a career ladder, enabling teachers to become master teachers and receive compensation for professional service to their colleagues. As a result of fresh thinking, excellence in teaching was acknowledged and rewarded, and district resources were used more efficiently.

Restructuring Leadership

The superintendent has been transforming the nature of district leadership from authoritarian regulation to decision making based on consensus. "The leadership is totally different than it was ... The culture has changed; the norms are different. I see myself as first among equals," she says. For example, the traditional norm dictates that the superintendent does not talk to teachers, but that norm no longer applies in Allentown. "Central office people as well as the superintendent are approachable by any person, at any level of the system."

She believes that principals themselves have learned that when they call the central office, the answer is not "no," but "let's see what we can do to help you through it." The schools have come to view the central office as support and resource instead of regulator.

The superintendent supports distributed leadership to enable all staff in the system to take responsibility for the success of each child. She states, "I want the prime leader of the building to be able to develop a resource of leadership, so that at any one time people who are not the principal are coming up with creative ideas and implementing them." The school that arranged the district-union waiver has witnessed the principal's personal and professional leadership style change from authoritarian to collaborative and supportive.

The Partnership Today

As foundation officials had hoped, the SCCC is becoming the "engine for change in the district," an advocate for SBM and restructuring that monitors schools, the district, and the superintendent to keep reform on course. The SCCC acts as oversight committee, sustaining the process when no foundation consultants are present and coordinating schools' requests for technical assistance. A subcommittee structures each year's reform efforts around two annual events, the summer restructuring workshop and a planning retreat. Principals insist on participating in this retreat because they have come to realize its significance.

The district has begun to look more systematically at the future and plan for continuing reform. In 1994 it held a series of Vision Forums, and as a result the Allentown school board approved a vision and a mission as official policy. The process also included a foundation-supported board retreat to translate the vision into objectives and practical standards, strategies for implementation, and meaningful indicators for measuring success.

■

The strength of the foundation's partnerships depends greatly
upon direct and ongoing pressure for restructuring.

The district has made a commitment to professional staff development that did not exist prior to the partnership. It has dramatically increased the budget allocated to this function and established its Center for Teaching and Learning, a professional development center dedicated to whole-school change.

Allentown is now playing a role in state and national reform efforts, leading the establishment of a new League for Educational Advancement in Pennsylvania (LEAP), a network of districts supporting systemic change for improved student learning. The district has been invited to become one of a limited number belonging to the National Education Association's National Center for Innovation. The Community Training and Assistance Center in Boston has accepted Allentown into its network of reforming districts.

The work of foundation consultants at Central Elementary School in Allentown illustrates the way Panasonic works to develop the capacity of school personnel to help themselves.

Central was a school clearly having difficulty. As stated in *P³*, the foundation's newsletter (Spring 1995), "Student performance data were low, and faculty morale was even lower. Staff members tried in vain to get parents involved in the school. Anger and frustration erupted as staff members fought with one another in meetings." A variety of efforts to improve the situation had not succeeded, including changes in leadership and staff and professional workshops for teachers. Yet the foundation was able to help.

A Panasonic consultant visited the school for several days in the spring of 1994 and helped staff define their problems. It became clear that they cared deeply about their students, but there was little trust among the faculty, with the principal, or with the district. They wanted to be working better among themselves and with students, but they did not know how to reverse their course. They wanted leadership, although they were reluctant to give authority to anyone. "They had to step outside their history and take new risks. But they were ready to take this step" (*P³*, Spring 1995).

Following some team building and work on the process they would use, 25 teachers redesigned the school reading program. They chose this as the vehicle for improvement because it was so central to the school, it affected all students and instruction in almost all subjects, and it involved everyone in the building. They also did something they hadn't thought of before: they convinced the staff who did not participate in the workshop that the plan was worth doing.

The reading program they developed combines a number of different elements, including cross-grade multiage grouping, block scheduling, heterogeneous and homogeneous learning groups (at different times and for different purposes), pull-out and pull-in programs for students with special needs, integrated regular and special programs, and some team teaching.

Ongoing work on the reading program takes a variety of forms. Teachers are examining their basic curriculum and beliefs about learning to read; defining grade-level expectations together to promote the articulation of the program across grades; and defining common instructional practices using a survey on how teachers conduct reading instruction. They established a steering committee to manage development and implementation of the program, and they developed a school in-service program, using district experts to help them learn new methods.

With Panasonic's guidance and critical friendship in the form of consultants who both prod the staff to be reflective and help solve problems, the school and faculty are changing. They have overcome internal dissension to provide leadership and developed a common vision to guide them.

They now anticipate and attempt to solve their own problems. For example, the school decided to send three teams to the 1995 summer workshops, each pursuing a separate topic. Knowing that these smaller teams would be less representative, the school asked these questions: What message does everyone need to give these teams before they do their work? How will we act on their work when we return to school in the fall?

Panasonic created an expectation that improvement should originate in the school. It helped by being there on an ongoing basis, which allowed the faculty to know and trust the consultants; bringing a number of options before the faculty to consider; facilitating the development of a process and positive school climate; and participating in the process as a critical friend rather than an outsider or central office person.

(continued on page 102)

The school must now add to and refine the elements of the reading program, for example, by integrating reading with the rest of language arts. Teachers need to find new and better ways to assess student performance and program development, and they must stay the course long enough for the developmental effects on students to show in their performance. Their success has been in the development of the school as a team effort.

Sustaining Momentum in the Most Fully Developed Partnership

How can the partnership sustain the momentum for reform? The strength of the foundation's partnership with Allentown still depends greatly upon its exerting direct and ongoing pressure for restructuring, building on the following accomplishments:

- The school board has demonstrated its commitment to reform, even when this meant changing its own policies and practices.

- The superintendent received the first "Penn Educator of the Year Award" from the University of Pennsylvania in the fall of 1993, after her first year in office, for having "demonstrated unusual involvement and commitment in identifying and helping to resolve school problems and current issues in education."

- The Allentown Education Association has become an even stronger proponent of restructuring and educational improvement efforts than it was when it developed the Allentown Accord.

- Allentown schools have taken major steps toward improvement: they are structured around school councils and use governance and decision-making structures that give a significant voice to teachers and parents.

- The SCCC, which is separate from both individual schools and the central office, provides opportunities to sustain the momentum and to address the issues being identified there.

- Both the Allentown Leadership Alliance and the Rider-Pool Foundation have the potential to provide necessary resources to support systemic change efforts, and both have the power to assist the district in developing support among business and community constituents.

The superintendent claims there is a "new culture of trust in the district, a heightened awareness and excitement in the schools and community," which has eroded traditional barriers between schools. For instance, the SCCC designed and carried out a highly symbolic event called TEAM (Together Everyone Achieves More) to kick off the 1993–94 school year, stimulating cohesion across the district by involving every employee in the system.

There is every reason to believe that Allentown will be able to sustain the momentum. Although the SCCC has not yet developed the capacity to replace the foundation, in order to sustain the reform process beyond the partnership Panasonic is helping the SCCC study itself and define its role in the ongoing development of the district.

The district, school board, and broader community agree with Panasonic about the ultimate goal in Allentown—"to have all students engaged in learning so they can be successful members of society." With Panasonic's help, the superintendent would "like to empower all members of the school community, including students, by giving them the training and skills necessary to make good decisions which will eventually lead to an increase in student achievement." She says, "I want the schools to be so deeply involved in the shared decision-making process that they'll insist that the next superintendent have the same beliefs."

Chapter 6

Helping Others Revitalize Public Schooling

Diverse American urban school systems have been Panasonic Partners. Through its partnerships, foundation staff and consultants have learned and continue to learn about how to promote and support systemic educational reform.

The Panasonic Foundation's work over the past decade has focused on the improvement of education through successful school and district restructuring and instructional improvement. Its key strategy has been activist technical assistance within the framework of long-term partnerships. Through successes and disappointments, Panasonic's staff and consultants believe they have learned fresh and immediately applicable lessons about using their form of technical assistance to stimulate reform. An important purpose of this book has been to allow other philanthropic and technical assistance organizations involved in the improvement of American education to examine the Partnership Program strategy and consider if it might be adapted to their own efforts.

A fundamental insight gained in part from disappointments has been that some school systems that desperately seek assistance for restructuring may not be ready for it. A partnership launched prematurely will probably fail or struggle for years, largely wasting funds and—more importantly—invaluable professional time, expertise, and other resources. As Panasonic staff have repeatedly witnessed, without district-level support whatever changes are made are likely to be short-lived or at best will remain as vulnerable as any experimental innovation.

Consequently, organizations should attend to a set of preconditions for productive partnerships. Two of the most important factors in selecting Panasonic Partners are (1) the district's *readiness* for reform and (2) its understanding of the foundation's *expectations* for the partnership.

Readiness and expectations have become central elements in determining whether to form a Panasonic Partnership because the process entails active, sustained engagement in promoting fundamental change. Such an ambitious mutual commitment is extremely demanding. The foundation now insists that new partnerships be established upon clear and explicit mutual expectations, reflected in strong preliminary agreement with district leaders about the vision, goals, and processes for a long-term relationship. The district must be motivated to engage in the process of change. Since this approach represents a sharp departure from traditional grant making, the foundation urges its prospective partners to consider carefully whether they would be comfortable with this way of working.

Readiness

Panasonic continues to refine its unique site selection process—a "courtship" instead of a formal grant proposal—partly to ensure that prospective partners understand from the outset that their intentions must be serious. The prolonged courtship also helps Panasonic assess those policies and practices that could eventually be modified to support improved teaching and learning, and gives the district time to assess the foundation. It is a mutual "getting to know each other" process to help both sides decide whether to work together.

The primary factor in exploring a partnership is a commitment to engage in long-term collaboration for fundamental change *with the foundation*. In its "critical friend" role, when a fundamental principle of reform is at stake, Panasonic sometimes appears more critical than friendly. Foundation staff and consultants may become so involved with traditional system functions that district staff may feel threatened rather than supported.

At the heart of the courtship is a classic pattern: one partner seeks self-improvement, the other has a mission to reform school systems. But is the district that wants to reform willing to make the necessary commitments and sacrifices? Is the technical assistant willing to help the district address critical issues as both partners learn from the experience?

■

Some school systems that desperately seek assistance
for restructuring may not be ready for it.

The school district must understand that a commitment to build capacity for ongoing reform entails redeploying existing resources, rather than depending mainly on new resources. The potential partners must mutually agree that this is a top priority visible to everyone in the school community. The partnership must be seen as central rather than ancillary—the system's primary engine to change itself. The partnership cannot serve as a complement to the existing system or as a means to strengthen and preserve it.

The foundation's negotiations are then dedicated to exploring and testing the sincerity of the district's professed commitment to comprehensive systemic reform. How fully do they realize what it will take to restructure their entire educational system and redesign the patterns of decision making, policies, practices, and relationships that shape it? The foundation knows from experience that systemic change is bound to be more complex and difficult than any formal agreement can capture in words.

At the same time, the district must assess how committed the foundation is to maintaining a long-term relationship. It is important for district staff to trust the foundation and the potential of a partnership.

The foundation does not engage in a partnership until it feels reasonably sure that all parties have made a commitment to fundamentally alter the school district's approach to its mission. Panasonic's hard-earned understanding of the demands of long-term restructuring means that no school district enters into a partnership without adequate understanding of what is likely to be involved.

Top-level decision makers, especially the superintendent and others who set and carry out school system policies and practices, must make a commitment to fundamental change. As the Santa Fe and Allentown Partnerships illustrate, however, Panasonic staff and consultants have come to appreciate deeply that changing formal structures and official roles is only part of the task, often the easiest part. Far more daunting are the challenges of altering the informal system policies and practices anchored in tradition, culture, and ingrained habits. Over time, the foundation hopes to witness certain kinds of change:

> We like to see that there is change, that people are thinking and trying different things. We need to have it clarified where the board stands, whether there is consensus within the board about a direction. The central office—not just the superintendent, but other people—must be committed to it and have the capacity to work with schools, to push and help. And the community must not just support the schools, but must become the outside force that supports reform in a constructive way, so that a different superintendent or a different board member isn't going to change the direction of the district or the reform.

> —Executive Director

Drawing on nearly a decade of intense experience with partnerships—some of them relatively successful, a few of them still-born—Panasonic staff and consultants are acutely aware of what it takes to provoke, support, and sustain change. They realize that the personal and professional investments of all parties involved are as significant as the foundation's institutional investments. Much of the experience is gratifying, as consultants and staff encourage, provide resources, link people and institutions, open dialogue, provoke reflection, and support initiatives.

On the other hand, much of the foundation's work can be enervating, as consultants and staff attempt to overcome deeply entrenched obstacles and dogged resistance to institutional change. The foundation's staff, consultants, and board of directors realize today what they could not have seen when they first agreed to work with Santa Fe—that entering a partnership amounts to a decision to commit one's professional life in a new arena.

Expectations

In assessing the likelihood that a partnership will succeed, Panasonic emphasizes its expectation that the partners will collaborate to accomplish the following major outcomes:

- All students achieving at high levels

- Practitioners informed and reflective, at all levels

- System policies and practices that actively stimulate, support, and sustain school-based, whole-school reform

A central element of successful partnership is that both partners regularly reflect on their work and reaffirm shared beliefs, values, and goals. The partners must clarify essential conditions for restructuring, reflecting roles and contributions of each partner and taking care to make needed adjustments in roles, actions, or commitments.

As a partnership begins, these expectations may be unfamiliar to district staff, or their practical implications may come as a surprise to some who had thought they understood the terms of the agreement. Panasonic's cautions and explanations notwithstanding, during the negotiations and early stages of a partnership, district officials rarely appreciate the full significance of what they are getting into.

For example, the school board, superintendent, and individual schools may endorse the principle that "all children can learn" while habitually following policies and practices that violate the concept. One of Panasonic's functions as "critical friend" is to point out such contradictions and encourage partners to resolve them. This may entail challenging certain cherished traditions, such as tracking, that enjoy strong constituencies.

■

During the negotiations and early stages of a partnership,
district officials rarely appreciate the full significance
of what they are getting into.

Exploring the contradiction between an educational philosophy based on equity and opportunity for all students and policies or practices such as tracking reveals several avenues for educational reform. But it also animates formidable resistance—not only in pockets here and there, but often throughout a school system—when traditional centers of power and influence feel genuinely threatened.

Panasonic's task in each partnership is to foster systemic conditions in which everyone in the school system—from school board president to teacher aide—mobilizes to support improved teaching and learning. As examples in the partnership stories have shown, schoolpeople themselves do not always share or fully understand the foundation's unswerving focus on comprehensive restructuring. Some participants would say that they are still puzzled as to why, for instance, Panasonic would support teacher visits to middle schools in another city as a stimulus to restructuring, yet flatly decline a request by dedicated, well-informed teachers for support in revamping the math curriculum because that would not promote restructuring.

Understanding the meaning of restructuring in practice requires a difficult conceptual transition among schoolpeople. Especially in the early stages of a partnership, the foundation repeatedly communicates the reform agenda through as many lenses as possible so that the entire district can gradually come to understand what restructuring means—and does not mean—in practice.

This communication process begins with the signature event, such as the Super Saturday—itself the result of a lengthy negotiation process. Panasonic typically launches a partnership with a frontal assault on conventional ways of organizing education and traditional ways that teachers and administrators plan and conduct their daily professional lives. A school district's successful negotiation of a Panasonic Partnership as a concerted effort toward systemic change depends mainly on the district's willingness to get involved intimately for many years with a no-nonsense team of educators intent on genuine reform. Once understandings are established and commitments are made, both partners must keep focused on partnership goals and assess progress toward achieving them.

Keeping Focused

Panasonic's goal in each of its partnerships is to change the way schools define and implement their mission, goals, and objectives. Just as the aim of teaching should be to create optimal conditions for learning—where all children can achieve to the best of their abilities—the foundation's purpose is to help the district and community cultivate conditions in which restructuring can flourish and support the development of schools using "best practices" to educate all students.

Information about research-based "best practices" is available to partners through a nationwide network of human resources. The difficulty lies in how to disseminate, establish, and refine effective practices, reliable knowledge, and methods of adaptation. The approach that the foundation initiated in Santa Fe involves reducing teachers' and administrators' isolation, increasing exposure to fresh ideas and tested methods, and connecting local educators directly to sources outside their limited institutional boundaries.

Panasonic's approach to systemic change reflects its belief that all schools can improve to the point where they resemble the best schools, by learning, adopting, and adapting research-based best practices with support, assistance, and provocation from their districts. The foundation believes that all students can learn at higher levels and that schools must aim to achieve this.

Panasonic seeks to move each partner toward support of best practices at the classroom level. The foundation fosters "teacher empowerment" in the belief that teachers fully informed of educational options and authorized to make instructional decisions will choose best practices. This is why, to the extent possible, the development of best practices is initiated and led by teachers themselves: they must understand, test, adapt, endorse, and implement those practices—replacing what they have customarily practiced, sometimes ingrained for decades—to improve the quality of interactions between teachers and children. Such a shift in perspective and practice requires collaborative governance and decision making, reinforced by constant exposure to sufficient information and exemplary practice.

How do the partners—both the foundation and the district—know when they are making progress toward systemic and school restructuring? The foundation understands that the relationship between systemic reform and student performance is indirect and complex, and that significant change becomes apparent only over time and with sustained effort. Even then the evidence does not generally surface in conventional forms, such as higher scores on standardized tests. In the long run, changes must become apparent in patterns of daily behavior—the ways in which administrators in school buildings or in the district organize priorities and make professional decisions, and the ways in which teachers adapt research-based best practices and appropriate assessment methods. Ultimately, the effects of structural reform become evident in daily activities of the individual school and classroom teacher.

Assessing the Partnerships

The impact of the foundation's partnership work has been described throughout this book—for example, in discussions about staff development and districtwide and school-based decision-making groups. These stories emerged from consultants' reports, interviews with partner staff, and an evaluation of the Partnership Program. In 1992 the foundation commissioned Education Resources Group (ERG) to help it more formally document the impact of the Partnership Program and to act as critical friend to the foundation in the same way the foundation acts as critical friend to its partner districts. ERG observed partnership activities and visited schools and classrooms in partner districts, and it surveyed teachers and students to determine what changes were occurring in teaching and learning practices over three years. Several clear findings emerged from this study:

- The level of activity around local systemic reform is directly related to the regularity of Panasonic's presence in the district.

- The expertise and contributions of foundation consultants who (1) nurture systemic reform and (2) provide professional development are critically important to the success of the partnerships.

- As a result of foundation-sponsored professional development, partnership schools are increasingly implementing "best" instructional practices that are considered critical in restructured schools by the larger educational community.

The Foundation's Presence

Systemic reform activities in partnership districts accelerated or slowed down depending on the regularity of visits by Panasonic consultants. A major thrust to help hire a new superintendent in Allentown in the winter and spring of 1992 was followed by a school year of less frequent visits, and district and school staff told ERG they felt "neglected." Lancaster, the newest partnership, has been progressing at a rapid pace with teams of Panasonic consultants present on a regular basis. The partnership in Minneapolis floundered with each of three new superintendents who were too busy to attend to it, yet it has been thriving for more than two years since the most recent superintendent turned to the foundation for assistance. Activity in San Diego was intense around middle schools in the early years, very quiet in 1992 and 1993, and increased once again as Panasonic consultants worked regularly with clusters of feeder schools. Most active in the first four to five years, the Santa Fe Partnership ended in 1995 when a new superintendent did not include the partnership in her plans.

For the foundation, this finding presents the challenge of weaning districts from a dependency on the partnership while developing self-sustaining and self-renewing systems. It is usually easier to simply provide resources than to develop resources within the learner.

Consultants' Contributions

Partnership districts rely heavily on the facilitating and resource roles of the foundation's consultants. The SCCC in Allentown looks to a senior consultant for guidance and leadership and to foundation-identified experts for its professional development institutes. After nearly a year of technical assistance and workshops by Panasonic consultants, most schools in Lancaster established school site councils as a first step toward implementing SBDM. Minneapolis designed a strategic plan for student assessment, focusing on nontraditional forms of assessment, with highly valued assistance from Panasonic-sponsored experts. San Diego's teachers association is now more engaged in reform after efforts by a senior consultant to establish better communication between the association and district leaders. Panasonic consultants were integrally involved in the design and development of a nationally recognized, innovative elementary school in Santa Fe.

Changes in Instructional Practices

Many instructional practices that are considered essential for restructured schools are used widely in partnership schools. More than 60 percent of teachers responding to surveys about their classroom practices use student *portfolios* (folders containing compilations of students' work) for instruction or assessment purposes. More than 80 percent of middle school teachers and half of high school teachers have planning time allocated for *interdisciplinary instruction*. Ninety percent of elementary school teachers focus on *problem solving* during instruction.

The health of the partnerships, as exemplified in these important findings, depends on many factors. Chief among them are the following:

- a district's desire to restructure, with the foundation as a partner;

- both partners sharing, or coming to share, common goals and agendas;

- the foundation maintaining a regular presence in the district, providing needed help when the district is ready to receive it; and

- assistance by experienced foundation consultants at several levels simultaneously: nurturing and supporting the superintendent, school board, and union leaders, for example, while also providing teachers with the professional development they need to change classroom practices.

Where these factors are present and real partnerships are formed, districts can build the capacity to continue restructuring on their own and to have powerful impacts on teachers and students.

Reflection and Renewal

The foundation's staff found ERG's evaluation results useful for reflection about the partnership experience, but it did not answer the many questions arising from that experience: Should we have gone into partnerships with term limits? Could we have been more specific about our expectations of the partners? Should we have had contracts or written agreements about specific benchmarks and expectations? Do "third party" assisters have to be from outside the community, and will other types of outsiders have the same leverage as a national foundation? What does successful systemic reform look like? To answer such questions, the foundation plans to (1) refine a draft set of templates for selection criteria, for engaging in a partnership, for assessing its progress, and for disengaging from it, and (2) commission a new evaluation study to assess the nature of the technical assistance approach and quality of assistance provided.

Templates for Future Work

Selection Criteria. The foundation has developed a set of critical areas it must explore and be comfortable about in its partnerships. These preconditions are that the district shares the foundation's beliefs, philosophy, and values; its student population includes substantial proportions of disadvantaged students; and its enrollment is at least 7,000 students. The district's potential to move toward systemic reform is grounded in the quality of its leadership, staff willingness and capacity to learn, state and local policy environments, and past reform efforts. Environmental and organizational stability and the financial resources required to develop a strong partnership are also considered.

Partnership Engagement Process. To formalize its periodic search for new partners, the foundation developed a "Request for Invitation" process that was implemented for the first time in the spring of 1996. Close to 200 school systems meeting the demographic preconditions of size and disadvantaged student population received letters from the foundation outlining the invitational process and a timeline for exploration and engagement in new partnerships. The main component of the process is the invitation package a district prepares, indicating a strong interest in participating in a partnership and providing information about its (1) vision and commitment to reform, (2) accomplishments and challenges in reform efforts to date, (3) resource and technical assistance needs, and (4) rationale for inviting a partnership. The foundation responds to these invitations via two-day fact-finding site visits, six-month explorations with districts clearly serious about forming a partnership, and formal two-year agreements with new partners.

Partnership Status Assessment. The foundation's Framework for School System Success (see Appendix B) delineates ten broad indicators for recognizing progress toward systemic reform. To measure attainment of these indicators, the foundation set up a template for ongoing assessment. A series of questions—including the following examples—provides the basis for examining partnership progress. Have short-term objectives been achieved? What is the strength of the partnership? Is the partnership having a significant impact on the district? Is the partner's capacity to sustain reform on its own increasing? Is the level of the foundation's investment in the partner appropriate for the work needed? These and related questions help the foundation make decisions about renewing two-year partnership agreements.

Partnership Disengagement Criteria. Partnerships end for a variety of reasons, some of which were discussed in earlier chapters. The foundation has learned that it may be more useful for both partners to purposefully disengage, for either positive or negative reasons. A successful partnership may end because eight or more Framework indicators have been achieved, resulting in sustainable or self-propelled reform. On the other hand, a partnership's health may be seriously affected by (1) a cataclysmic leadership change, (2) recognition that a "plateau" of change and achievement has been reached, or (3) decreasing viability due to less need, entry of other outside assisters, and/or increasing divergence between strategic interests of the partners. Both positive and negative disengagement criteria must be seriously examined before a partnership is ended.

These templates serve several purposes, but one of the most important is establishing for both partners standards and expectations that guide the relationship. They also provide each partner with an objective framework for making decisions about the usefulness and viability of the partnership, based primarily on measuring progress toward systemic reform. (The four templates are presented in Appendix C.)

Evaluating the Technical Assistance Strategy

Technical assistance is the linchpin and the strength of the Panasonic Partnership Program. It is clearly a successful strategy, and the foundation is ready to examine more deeply the specific nature and aspects of technical assistance that contribute to partnership progress.

The evaluation Panasonic currently envisions is focused on the effectiveness of technical assistance in bringing about systemic reform and developing the capacity of local educators to design and implement their own reform plans. It will determine if the use and deployment of consultants is efficient and effective within the parameters of foundation resources and goals. Finally, it will attempt to distinguish how the various forms of technical assistance (e.g., consultations with superintendents, board retreats, and on-site workshops) affect the progress of school reform.

The foundation expects to learn if the technical assistance approach is sound, and if partners perceive the technical assistance provided in the same way as Panasonic perceives it, in terms of usefulness and quality. This evaluation, which is expected to commence in early 1997, should help the foundation improve and renew the technical assistance it provides.

Prospects for Systemic Reform

Given the number and variety of efforts that have been made in the last two decades to reform American education, it seems foolhardy to predict that urban school systems will quickly change or that student outcomes will dramatically improve in the short term. Yet, following the progress of schools involved with the Panasonic Partnership Program does offer cause for optimism.

School districts and schools around the country are actively exploring forms of governance and decision making that give voice to professionals and school constituencies, and they are looking closely at their operating structures. They are questioning traditional approaches to organizing students for instruction, the use of classroom and professional time, the data they collect about student and school performance, and how changes in these and other aspects of school structure could improve school life and student achievement.

The Panasonic Foundation plans to maintain the Partnership Program, continuing and refining its work with current partners while identifying new partnerships. The foundation will also explore collaboration with other organizations attempting to help schools and districts improve.

American public education lies at a fascinating crossroads of opportunity. As a result of research in cognitive science on student learning and improvement efforts such as the Panasonic Partnership Program, educators now know more about how to improve student learning and organize schools to promote outstanding classroom practice than at any time in American history. The challenge now is to get this knowledge to teachers and school administrators and to help them make sense of and apply it. Panasonic will continue to meet the challenge with its partners, seeking ways to create exemplary schools and school development that can inform efforts across the country.

Sources

Education Resources Group. 1995. *Evaluation Report on the Panasonic Partnership Program, 1993–1995*. Princeton, NJ: Education Resources Group.

Holzman, M., and Tewel, K. 1992. The San Diego Panasonic Partnership: A Case Study in Restructuring. *Teachers College Record* 93(3): 488–99.

LeMahieu, P., and Mehrens, W.A. 1994. *Evaluation of the Minneapolis Public Schools' Evaluation and Testing Programs (Report to the Minneapolis Public Schools)*.

Middle Grades Assessment Program (Users and Leaders Manuals). 1984. Currboro, NC: Center for Early Adolescence.

Mitchell, P.B. 1990. *Report on the Evaluation of the Panasonic Foundation School Improvement Program: San Diego and Santa Fe*. Alexandria, VA: National Association of State Boards of Education.

Panasonic Foundation. 1996. *The Panasonic Foundation: We're About…* Secaucus, NJ: Panasonic Foundation.

———. 1995. *Every Student a Learner: Every School a Success*. Secaucus, NJ: Panasonic Foundation.

———. 1991. *Panasonic Foundation 1984–1990: Partners in Restructuring Schools*. Secaucus, NJ: Panasonic Foundation.

Sa, S. 1992. Another Partnership Goes to School: The Panasonic Foundation's School Restructuring Program. *Teachers College Record* 93(3): 463–71.

———. 1991. *The Need for Systemic School-Based School Reform*. Prepared for the U.S. Department of Education. Secaucus, NJ: Panasonic Foundation.

Sommerfield, M. 1994. Small Player, Big Plans. *Education Week*, 15 June, 25–27.

Senior Panasonic Foundation Consultants
1995–1996

Tom Corcoran is a senior research scientist and codirector of the Consortium for Policy Research in Education at the University of Pennsylvania. He is also a member of the team evaluating the National Science Foundation's State Systemic Initiative. He lives in Pennington, New Jersey.

LaVaun Dennett has worked as a national education consultant, a school administrator, magnet manager, parent, community activist, and teacher. As principal of Montlake Elementary School in Seattle, she led an exemplary educational restructuring initiative and received several awards in the process. She lives in Caldwell, Idaho.

Lawrence S. Feldman has been a Dade County (Florida) Public Schools employee since 1973. During those years he has worked as an exceptional education teacher, regular education teacher, assistant principal, principal, and regional office director. He lives in Miami.

Stephen Fink is assistant superintendent of the Edmonds School District in Washington. In his 20 years of experience he has also worked as a school principal, director of special programs, special education teacher, and consultant. He lives in Lynnwood, Washington.

David H. Florio, who is senior program consultant to the Panasonic Foundation, has been engaged in education reform and policy development for the National Academy of Sciences, the National Science Foundation, the U.S. Department of Education, and the American Federation of Teachers. During a nearly 30-year career, he has also been a teacher, university professor, association executive director, and government relations officer. He lives in Washington, D.C.

Andrew Gelber is an independent education consultant who was a founding staff member (1985-93) of PATHS/PRISM (now the Philadelphia Education Fund), one of the nation's first and largest public/private partnership organizations in support of public education reform. His work has also included designing and implementing professional development programs for teachers and principals. He lives in Philadelphia.

Gail Gerry is an independent education consultant who has previously worked as a teacher, principal, district-level curriculum director, researcher, assessment consultant, writer, and editor. Most recently, she was director of professional development in the Kentucky Department of Education. She lives in Louisville.

Michael Katims is a senior associate with the Center on Learning, Assessment, and School Structure. He has previously been a senior associate with Education Resources Group, an assistant superintendent of schools, and coordinator of professional development for public school educators. He lives in Princeton, New Jersey.

Stephen M. Ladd, an educator with 25 years of experience at a variety of levels—instructional aide, teacher, PRIDE specialist (Professional Resource in Developmental Education), assistant principal, and district-level administrator—is currently serving as the assistant superintendent of Beaverton School District in Beaverton, Oregon.

Patricia Bruce Mitchell is senior consultant for the State Education Improvement Partnership, which assists states engaged in systemic education reform through collaborative efforts of the Council of Chief State School Officers, Education Commission of the States, National Association of State Boards of Education, National Conference of State Legislators, and the National Governors' Association. She lives in Alexandria, Virginia.

Vicky Murray has been in education for more than 20 years. She has been an English teacher, assistant principal of both a junior high and high school, principal of a high school, and director of personnel. She is currently supervisor of middle school and high school principals of Bellevue School District in Bellevue, Washington. She lives in Seattle.

Robert W. Nolte, as senior associate with the Center for Leadership in School Reform, works with school districts and organizations pursuing restructuring on strategic planning, organizational development, and training development and implementation. He lives in West Hartford, Connecticut.

George S. Perry assists school districts and community groups in organizational development, strategic planning, professional development, and curriculum reform to better meet the needs of all students. He conducts research to help administrators and teachers improve practice. Mr. Perry has held positions in education policy and program management at the local, state, and national levels. He lives in Western Springs, Illinois.

Mitchell Sakofs, director of special projects for the Outward Bound National Headquarters, is an experiential education specialist and author of more than 30 articles and two books on the topic. Additionally, he is a consultant for the Connecticut Center for School Change. He lives in Fairfield, Connecticut.

Gladys Sheehan is an educational consultant who from 1975 to 1992 held several leadership posts in the Minneapolis Public Schools, including director of media services, administrator of staff development and media services, acting director of curriculum, and acting associate superintendent for curriculum and instruction. From 1989 until 1992 she served on the superintendent's cabinet. She lives in Minneapolis.

Kenneth J. Tewel, senior program advisor to the Panasonic Foundation, has filled numerous roles during 30 years of work in education: high school teacher, union leader, assistant principal, central office administrator, associate professor, and principal of three New York City high schools: Franklin K. Lane High School, George Westinghouse High School, and the nationally acclaimed Stuyvesant High School. He lives in Fort Lauderdale.

The Panasonic Foundation Framework for School System Success

A successful school system is driven by the belief that all students can learn at demanding levels. The principal function of the system is to enable each school to realize that belief. A successful system changes to meet goals and challenges and strives to attain the following attributes.

1. A Vision Focused on Equity and Learning for All

- The system shares a vision of ALL children learning content that is engaging, and succeeding at challenging levels.

- Learning standards define what ALL students should know and be able to do at each level of schooling: primary, intermediate, middle, and graduation.

- The community, parents, and staff, through an inclusive process, collaborate on the development and regular review of the standards.

- Practices relating to student work, curriculum, teaching, and assessment strategies, and the allocation of technologies enable all students to meet system learning standards.

- Students, regardless of background and differences in strengths and ways of learning, have multiple opportunities and means to demonstrate their knowledge.

2. **A Strategic Direction Based on Learning and the Centrality of the School as the Place of Learning**

- The system acts on the principle that each school, as the place of learning, has authority to design its own program to meet the system learning standards.

- Systemwide initiatives respect school agendas and decisions.

- The system has established a strategic direction, with short- and long-term goals, based on its vision, standards, and principles.

- The system has established indicators of a successful school focused on all students meeting the learning standards.

3. **Clear Delineation of Roles, Authority, and Responsibilities**

- *Students*, assisted by parents and other significant adults, prepare themselves for and actively participate in learning and respect the rights and well-being of all members of the school community.

- *Each school community*—teachers, principal, and other staff, with parent engagement—takes part in shared decision making to allocate budgets, select and assign personnel, choose materials, create schedules, and determine and implement curricular and teaching strategies within the system parameters based on system standards and direction.

- *Central office* coordinates resources, documents and communicates progress, facilitates school change, advocates for exemplary schools, and intervenes when schools do not enable children to learn.

- *The school board* sets broad policy, approves standards and the system budget, monitors system progress, generates community support, and employs the superintendent.

- *Systemwide leadership* establishes strategic direction and broad goals, maintains system focus, communicates direction and results, facilitates the change process, and engenders wide and deep support for the strategic direction.

4. **An Infrastructure That Enhances Professional and Organizational Capacity**

- The system maintains an infrastructure to provide high-quality, well-coordinated professional development and technical assistance that strengthens each school.

- Professional development and technical assistance resources are controlled by the school site, where appropriate.

- The system places high priority on identifying exemplary candidates for employment, orienting new staff, preparing all employees for changing roles, and building broad leadership capacity.

- Networks and technologies are used to link schools and teachers within and beyond the district.

- An advanced technology system assists professional learning; manages student, school, and system data; and connects schools and teachers with useful knowledge and exemplary practice.

- Business, education, and human service agency partnerships are part of the infrastructure and are aligned with the strategic direction of the system.

5. **Assessment and Evaluation Practices Aligned with Learning Standards and Strategic Direction**

- Student assessment strategies and practices represent widely trusted measures of progress directly aligned with system learning standards.

- A variety of assessment methods are used to measure the most important aspects of learning and provide all students appropriate opportunities to demonstrate their knowledge and skills.

- School evaluations are based on system indicators of school success that have been developed through a process involving each school community.

- Student assessment, school evaluation, and other indicators of system progress are focused on growth or value added over time.

6. **An Accountability System Focused on Results**

- The system as a whole and system units, including each school, are responsible and answerable for making progress toward system standards and goals.

- The system provides schools clear incentives and support, such that those making progress are nurtured and encouraged and those initiating reforms or requesting help receive needed assistance.

- The system applies clear consequences and intervention strategies, including restructuring and reconstitution, to schools that are unable to assure student learning.

- Incentives and consequences for system leaders and central office staff performance are clearly articulated, widely known, and aligned with the system standards and strategic direction.

- Employees and schools are responsible for reflecting on their performance, understanding and articulating their needs, and securing needed knowledge and assistance.

7. **Effective Use of Well-Managed Data**

- A comprehensive data management system is maintained to supply clear, timely, accurate, and useful information to schools, community, system leaders, and other policy makers.

- Student assessment, school indicator, and other data are used to construct school profiles to make informed decisions.

- The system gathers data only with a clear purpose and in a coordinated manner that is least burdensome to schools.

- Teachers, district and school-site administrators, and other staff regularly solicit input from a variety of sources to engage in reflection on individual and organizational performance.

8. An Effective Communications System

- The communications system uses multiple technologies, channels, and strategies to listen to and inform system participants and constituents.

- Effective interaction is maintained among and between teachers, schools, central office staff, system leaders, and constituents.

- Specific communications strategies address the challenges posed by disparate school sites, teacher and school isolation, diverse constituents, and multiple levels of education governance.

- The system is informed by and informs current and potential federal, state, and local policy decisions affecting its standards and strategic direction.

9. Teachers Unions and Other Professional Associations as Important System Components

- Unions/associations, as part of the system, help determine and actively work to implement the strategic direction.

- Union/association–management relations reflect mutual respect, a belief in shared decision making, and regular leadership dialogue.

- Contract policies and procedures support the strategic direction, effective professional practice, and school-based, shared decision making.

- Unions/associations, with broader system support, transform their culture and practice to reflect and promote members' changing professional roles.

10. Meaningful Engagement of System Constituents and the Broader Community

- Each school community and systemwide constituents meaningfully participate in the development and ongoing review of the system standards, vision, and direction.

- The system uses a variety of strategies and technologies to inform and engage parents and other constituents in the work of each school and of the system as a whole, with special attention to new parents.

- An enduring alliance of system constituents, based on clear individual and group responsibilities, engenders public understanding of and support for changes needed to achieve the strategic direction, and serves as a stable force to keep the system on course, particularly during periods of political or leadership transition.

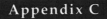

Four Templates for Partnerships

> ## Selection Criteria and Variables for New Partnership Sites
> *(Entry Framework)*
>
> ### 1. Preconditions
>   a. Shares foundation objectives and values:
>   - all children can learn
>   - school-based decision making
>   - systemic restructuring
>
>   b. Student demographics—includes substantial proportions of disadvantaged
>
>   c. Student population in district of at least 7,000
>
> ### 2. Potential for real movement toward Framework attributes
>   a. Quality of leadership (board, superintendent, union, and/or community)
>
>   b. Willingness and capacity to learn
>
>   c. Policy context (state policy environment will allow change)
>
>   d. Past history of reform efforts and outside partners
>
> (continued on page 134)

3. Potential for strong partnership (using "Strength of Foundation-Partner Relationship" template)

4. Environmental and organizational stability

5. Strategic interest of foundation

   a. Potential risks and benefits to PF

   b. Expands R&D knowledge to PF and to field—overall or in specific Framework area(s)

   c. "Fit" with overall PF portfolio and/or adds diversity

   - size
   - location (including ease of access)
   - level of system (district, state, intermediate unit)

6. Level of funding and time commitment needed and/or potential for leverage

Engagement Process
(Progressional Development)

1. Identification through "Request for Invitations"
   a. Meets demographic and size criteria

   b. Expresses real interest in and understanding of restructuring

   c. Sense of "fit" with PF gestalt

2. Initial assessment using Entry Framework
   On-site fact finding: two to three consultants, two to three days

3. Six to eight months further exploration*
   a. Mutually agreed-upon "project"/initiative

   b. Consultation

4. Initial two-year investment*
   a. Mutual agreement regarding goals/objectives, resource commitment

   b. Joint development of benchmarks, timelines, assessment mechanisms

5. Long-term commitment in two-year increments*

* Assessment, using "Partnership Assessment" template regarding potential for progress, actual achievements, etc., to be conducted at end of every stage, with reports to be shared with site.

A. Progress Assessment

1. Have the short-term objectives been achieved? Is there progress? Why/Why not?

2. Does the partner (district, superintendent, board, union, other leaders) understand the content of the partnership work (the what and why)? Does the foundation? What's the evidence?

3. Does the partner understand the process of the work (the how)? Does the foundation? What's the evidence?

4. Does the partner "walk the talk"? Does the foundation? What's the evidence?

5. What is the strength of the partnership? (See part B below.)

6. Does the partner attend to the totality of the Framework?

7. What is the foundation's strategic position in the site (is PF's influence merely peripheral)? What's the evidence?

8. Does the partner make a contribution to the foundation's strategic interests? How?

9. Is the partner's capacity to sustain reform on its own increasing? What's the evidence?

10. Is there expansion of the number of individuals, groups, organizations involved in the reform/partnership work?

11. What have been the most significant successes of the partnership (this year, to date)?

12. What have been the most persistent problems for the partnership (this year, to date)?

B. Strength of Foundation-Partner Relationship (to be assessed by both foundation and partner stakeholders, using a four-point scale)

1. Level of trust between foundation and partner (at various levels: school, central office, board, union, community, etc.)
2. Level of candor/openness
3. Depth of common understanding
4. Clarity of mutual expectations
5. Follow-through on commitments (two-way)
6. Importance/value of partnership ("central" vs. "marginal")
   a. at school level
   b. to union
   c. at central office level
   d. etc.
7. Importance of restructuring to the partner
8. Focused on the Framework

Disengagement Factors

A. Positive

1. Preponderance of "8"–"10" on Framework (see Appendix B)
2. Sustainable and self-propelled reform process
3. Goals attained

B. Negative

1. Decreasing strength of partnership (based on four-point scale)
2. Achievement plateau
3. Fundamental shift in district direction
4. Irreconcilable differences among key stakeholders

C. Positive or Negative

1. Decreasing need for foundation (e.g., through entry of other helpers)
2. No longer meets foundation's portfolio criteria
3. Duration of partnership
4. Cumulative investment by foundation

Where the Panasonic Foundation Has Worked

Allentown School District (PA)*

Boston Public Schools (MA)**

Boulder Valley Public Schools (CO)

Broward County Public Schools (FL)*

Cincinnati Public Schools (OH)*

Corpus Christi Independent School District (TX)**

Dade County Public Schools (FL)

East Baton Rouge Parish School System (LA)

Elizabeth Public Schools (NJ)

Englewood Public Schools (NJ)

Flint Community Schools (MI)**

Hayward Unified School District (CA)**

School District of Lancaster (PA)*

Maine State Department of Education

Minneapolis Public Schools (MN)*

Minnesota State Department of Education

New Jersey State Department of Education

New Mexico State Department of Education*

Northern New Mexico Network for Rural Education*

Norwalk–La Mirada Unified School District (CA)**

Pasco County Florida Schools**

Providence Public Schools (RI)**

Rhode Island State Department of Education

Rochester City School District (NY)

San Diego City Schools (CA)*

Santa Fe Public Schools (NM)

Seattle Public Schools (WA)

Somerville Public Schools (MA)

William Penn School District (PA)

*Current Partnership sites (January 1997)

**Current Exploratory Partnership sites (January 1997)

Assessment

Authentic assessments (also referred to as alternative, performance, and portfolio assessments): Methods of evaluating students' learning through demonstrations of progress toward academic goals, instead of (or sometimes in addition to) norm-referenced standardized achievement tests with multiple-choice questions. In authentic assessment, teachers review student portfolios (i.e., compilations of students' academic, artistic, and other work), multimedia presentations, and performances, which are based on important, real-life problems.

Performance assessment: Evaluation of students' learning through measures of how well they actively demonstrate or "perform" acquisition of knowledge and skills; for example, they can make project demonstrations (e.g., a scientific experiment) to teachers, fellow students, and others, or present analytical materials and findings based on a long-term research project.

Portfolio assessment: A form of assessment in which students collect and organize examples of academic and artistic accomplishments completed over time, in order to demonstrate the content and processes of their progress toward academic and expressive goals and objectives.

Standardized test: An instrument, usually a timed paper-and-pencil test, which measures academic knowledge and skills, e.g., the Scholastic Assessment Test (SAT). It often features multiple-choice items scored according to statistical norms that compare responses among large samples of students to similar or identical questions.

Curriculum

Integrated: Two or more distinct subjects, such as mathematics and science, which are traditionally isolated in presentation of content, organization, time of day, and location, are unified through combinations of related elements.

Interdisciplinary: Academic activities involving the simultaneous or sequential study of topics and perspectives drawn from and often combining two or more fields, e.g., social studies that integrates history, the arts, and literature.

Thematic: Subject matter is organized and taught around common topics or related ideas. For example, individualism or leadership in social studies/history; the struggle for freedom in American literature; or theories (e.g., waves and particles; chemical reactions) in science.

Traditional: Curricula organized around the major academic subjects characterizing classical education: e.g., mathematics, history, language arts (English), science.

Educational Reform

Restructuring: The redesign of the fundamental governance/operating relationships throughout a whole school or a public school system that influence conditions for effective learning among all students. The outcome, a desired improvement of teaching and learning, grows from a consensus around new priorities reflected in reorganization of responsibilities, roles, and lines of authority.

School improvement programs/strategies: Specific interventions designed to improve the quality of teaching and learning in an individual school or in specific schools treated separately rather than in schools across a school district.

Systemic reform: The focus of restructuring efforts upon the entire system of a public school district in addition to individual schools. This term is also used by some researchers to mean alignment of standards, curriculum, and assessment.

Instruction

"Best practices" in instruction: Approaches and specific methods of teaching that embody proven, research-based knowledge that fosters effective conditions for learning.

Block scheduling: Organization of instruction into blocks of time lasting significantly longer (e.g., 90 minutes or 2 hours) than the traditional and relatively small units (periods) of 45 to 50 minutes, permitting intensive or extended learning activities, including group projects, field trips, interdisciplinary teaching, and individualized writing development.

Cooperative learning: Organization of heterogeneously grouped students into small, mixed-ability learning teams in which students share responsibility for ensuring that (1) everyone in the group masters an assigned task or skill, or (2) each individual is able to make a meaningful contribution toward a collective goal. In practice, many tracked classrooms also use cooperative learning teams. The teachers' role is to present a lesson, assign students to work in cooperative learning groups, and then teach individual groups as necessary.

Inclusion: The policy and practice of serving students who are normally assigned to special education classes in a regular education classroom, with in-class support. Inclusion resembles the broader term "mainstreaming" (widely used in the 1980s) but differs in its more specific focus. One important purpose of inclusion is to prevent stereotyping, low expectations, and social isolation often associated with special needs students. Inclusion is implemented at varying times and for different purposes, depending upon several factors such as scheduling, type of activity, adaptability of curriculum and instructional methods, and expertise of the teacher or teachers.

Manipulatives-based math instruction: The use of a wide variety of tangible materials (manipulatives), such as blocks and rods of different sizes and colors, that children can arrange to create and discover mathematical concepts and relationships. This approach, used especially with elementary school students, reflects research and theory on cognitive development confirming that many children can best learn mathematical concepts through direct experience with concrete rather than abstract representations.

Pull-out/pull-in programs: The practice of withdrawing (pull-out) or bringing in (pull-in) students for instruction for different purposes and at different times. The most well-known pull-out programs have been for special instruction to economically disadvantaged and/or poorly performing students (Title I). Increasing inclusion of special education students in regular classrooms (also called mainstreaming) or a range of other students into discrete classes, units, or projects illustrate pull-in programs.

Team teaching: Organizing and coordinating instruction by two or more teachers—language arts and social studies, for instance—permitting and encouraging cross-fertilization of concepts, skills, and activities. Can also refer to teaming up of "regular" and "special" education teachers to instruct a classroom of both typical children and those with disabilities.

Whole language: A process for teaching reading and writing that provides materials and instruction that are meaningful to the learner, i.e., they are "whole" and they contain meaningful language. The whole language teacher plans experiences, activities, interactions, and a classroom environment that supports individualized, active literacy development. Children are immersed in both spoken and written languages, listening, speaking, reading, writing, and meaningful communications. In more traditional reading instruction, teachers use a preplanned, sequential skills approach that treats all children the same. Although phonics is usually included in traditional reading instruction, many whole language teachers also teach phonics.

Middle School Philosophy

A movement among schools that serve adolescent students between the ages traditionally associated with elementary and high school grades. The philosophy embraces and refines a coherent body of research on (1) values and principles of school organization and (2) curricula and instructional methods focusing on the distinctive social and academic learning needs of early adolescents. The "philosophy" is applied in an institution with a particular identity—one that is neither an extension of elementary schooling nor a "junior" high school. As the number and variety of such schools have proliferated, the movement has gained strength, confidence, and respectability among professional educators, especially those who endorse the educational policies and practices evident in middle schools.

Models of School Reform

Coalition of Essential Schools: A nationwide network of member schools (mostly secondary) dedicated to educational principles (e.g., students should learn to use their minds well), originally articulated under the leadership of Theodore Sizer of Brown University. In addition to subscribing to a common set of ideas and values, the network exchanges resources and information, fosters collegial relationships among its member schools and individual teachers and administrators, and provides professional development activities for school staff. Re: Learning is a state-level effort linked to the Coalition of Essential Schools that provides a range of resources for school reforms that are consistent with Coalition principles and methods.

Comer Model: Yale University psychologist James Comer's School Development Program is often referred to as the Comer Model. It is a strategy for school improvement that is based on the belief that academic achievement of children is inseparable from their social and psychological development. In "Comer" schools parents and teachers play an active role in school governance, and a mental health team is organized to provide guidance to teachers and to the school governance team on child-development issues.

Effective Schools Movement: An early 1980s movement among education strategists and practitioners that focused policies, interventions (such as special funding), and technical assistance upon discrete characteristics of schools that research indicated would create conditions for effective academic learning among all students, regardless of socioeconomic class. The five discrete characteristics include strong administrative leadership, orderly school climate, emphasis on a school's main academic agenda, high expectations for student achievement, and ongoing monitoring of student progress.

School-Based or Site-Based Decision Making

Participatory management: Involvement of all constituency groups, including the principal, teachers, other staff, community members, parents, and even students, in decision making.

School-based budgeting: Locating at the level of the individual school the responsibility for design and management of budgetary categories, priorities, and methods of implementation and accountability.

School-based management: Concentrating maximum decision-making authority about programs, personnel, and budgets at the level of the individual school rather than the central office of the school district.

School site councils: Decision-making bodies made up of a widely representative group of individuals responsible for determining the priorities and management of an individual school. For example, a council might select and hire the school principal and develop the school's statement of educational philosophy and mission.

Student Grouping

Heterogeneous grouping versus tracking: The organization of students into groups representing a wide range of abilities rather than into "tracks," i.e., strictly defined categories of academic abilities, often determined by standardized test scores.

Interdisciplinary teams: Organization of students into groups and subgroups—"teams" designed to foster cooperation and collaboration around common objectives and goals. Such teams, often made up of 100 to 125 students with a group of four core-subject teachers, are developed to promote information sharing, build and reinforce social and academic skills, and enlist a range of group resources to address goals and objectives involving more than one academic discipline.

Multiage classrooms: Organization of classes or school grades into groups of students of different ages, (e.g., a combined fourth-fifth grade), who would traditionally have been assigned to grades determined by specific age ranges.

Teacher Empowerment

Efforts to promote ability and capacity of teachers to develop, organize, and manage curriculum and instruction and foster collegial professional relationships, made possible by policies, administrative practices, and resources provided within and throughout a school.

Technical Assistance

Providing expertise either necessary or especially useful to achieve goals and objectives of educational reform and professional development. Technical assistance especially includes the regular presence of consultants dedicated to provoking fundamental questions, supporting initiatives, exposing and generating options, and helping to sustain changes over a period of years. It may take the following forms: workshops, expert consultation, school staff retreats for planning and evaluation, special experts in a particular field such as student assessment or budgeting, and introduction of external resources such as curricular materials.

Index

Terry A. Clark

T erry Clark is president and cofounder of Education Resources Group, Inc. (ERG), a nonprofit firm that seeks to assist reform and influence policy in education and social services through evaluation, documentation, research, technical assistance, and training. ERG moved from New York City to Princeton, NJ, in 1994.

During two decades of experience in research and evaluation of school improvement programs and other innovations, Dr. Clark has worked directly with major philanthropies and universities, large city school systems, and national and regional nonprofit institutions. She has been an advisor to the Ford and Panasonic Foundations and the U.S. Department of Education, senior research scientist and adjunct faculty member at New York University, and director of research for the New York City Board of Education. She is a member of the Board of Directors of the High/Scope Educational Research Foundation and the Editorial Board of the Social and Institutional Analysis Section of the *American Educational Research Journal*.

Dr. Clark has written numerous articles and monographs about school improvement, school dropout prevention, and documentation as a form of evaluation. Her graduate degrees are in educational administration from the University of Pennsylvania, and she resides in Princeton with her husband and her daughter, Annie.

Richard A. Lacey

Richard Lacey has been a consultant and professional writer and editor in education, employment, and job training since 1977. His articles and other publications cover a range of issues in policy analysis, school improvement, and institutional change, frequently aimed at practitioners.

He holds undergraduate and graduate degrees from Yale and the University of Massachusetts. After serving five years on the public education staff of the Ford Foundation, Dr. Lacey headed a K–12 independent school and consulted and wrote frequently about educational reform and youth employment. In 1985 he cofounded Pierce Kennedy Hearth (PKH), a management services firm based in Connecticut.

Dr. Lacey has testified before congressional committees, served on numerous task forces on education and youth employment, and led successful nationwide coalitions of organizations promoting increased educational and employment opportunities for economically disadvantaged groups. He lives in New York City with his wife and his teenage son, Alexander.